John Adams

A Captivating Guide to an American Founding Father Who Served as the Second President of the United States of America

© Copyright 2019

All Rights Reserved. No part of this book may be reproduced in any form without permission in writing from the author. Reviewers may quote brief passages in reviews.

Disclaimer: No part of this publication may be reproduced or transmitted in any form or by any means, mechanical or electronic, including photocopying or recording, or by any information storage and retrieval system, or transmitted by email without permission in writing from the publisher.

While all attempts have been made to verify the information provided in this publication, neither the author nor the publisher assumes any responsibility for errors, omissions or contrary interpretations of the subject matter herein.

This book is for entertainment purposes only. The views expressed are those of the author alone, and should not be taken as expert instruction or commands. The reader is responsible for his or her own actions.

Adherence to all applicable laws and regulations, including international, federal, state and local laws governing professional licensing, business practices, advertising and all other aspects of doing business in the US, Canada, UK or any other jurisdiction is the sole responsibility of the purchaser or reader.

Neither the author nor the publisher assumes any responsibility or liability whatsoever on the behalf of the purchaser or reader of these materials. Any perceived slight of any individual or organization is purely unintentional.

Free Bonus from Captivating History (Available for a Limited time)

Hi History Lovers!

Now you have a chance to join our exclusive history list so you can get your first history ebook for free as well as discounts and a potential to get more history books for free! Simply visit the link below to join.

Captivatinghistory.com/ebook

Also, make sure to follow us on Facebook, Twitter and Youtube by searching for Captivating History.

Contents

INTRODUCTION 1

CHAPTER 1 – JOHN ADAMS: POLITICAL ACTIVIST 4

CHAPTER 2 – FROM COUNSEL TO PATRIOT 13

CHAPTER 3 – THE SECOND CONTINENTAL CONGRESS 21

CHAPTER 4 – JOHN ADAMS: DIPLOMAT & CONSTITUTIONALIST 32

CHAPTER 5 – JOHN ADAMS: VICE PRESIDENT AND THEN PRESIDENT UNDER THE NEW CONSTITUTION 44

CHAPTER 6 – TO FIGHT OR NOT TO FIGHT: THE QUASI-WAR 54

CHAPTER 7 – 1800: THE POLITICS OF DISSENSION 61

CHAPTER 8 – JOHN ADAMS: HIS THOUGHTS AND RETIREMENT 66

CONCLUSION 73

REFERENCES 79

Introduction

John Adams once wrote, "People and nations are forged in the fires of adversity." That was very much Adams' experience. Although he was often maligned, he didn't deserve it. Having been born in the English colony of Massachusetts in 1735, he not only witnessed a new nation emerging from the shell of infancy, but he also participated in its growing pains. Adams was a man who was frequently asked to assume roles in which he had little experience, like that of a diplomat to France and England. In a sense, he was a part of the vanguard that the government had thrown into the fray.

But why would the government choose him to represent their interests? Perhaps the main reason was that John Adams was a lawyer and understood the legal significance of treaties and agreements. He was also a simple and objective man who knew how to get to the heart of an issue in quick order. However, the French and British were confused by his direct approach. They preferred charm decorated with solicitousness and obsequiousness, and Adams often had to tread water. Even his wife was criticized because her gowns weren't up to the standards of the nobility she encountered there. The one quality he had that aided him well during these times was the fact that he was tough and not easily discouraged. He threw all his energy into a task in order to serve his country.

John Adams was a deep thinker unless his ire was aroused. Generally, he tried to resolve the issues that most annoyed him. Unlike a lot of the other hot-headed Patriots during his time, Adams was well aware of his shortcomings. When asked to write the Declaration of Independence, he said, "I am obnoxious, suspected and unpopular." No doubt the members of the Continental Congress chuckled at that. Adams kept no secrets when it came to the way he felt, especially when it came to British officials. Even British General William Howe was made aware of this when Adams leaped up and led his delegation out of the room when he realized that Howe tried to resolve the Revolutionary War without the authority to draw up a treaty.

Historians have cast aspersions on Adams for conducting the secret XYZ Affair because it was ineffective. However, he was cheered in the streets of Philadelphia after telling the country that he turned down France's bid for peace because America was expected to offer generous bribes to French Foreign Minister Talleyrand in exchange for no interference in American shipping. Because he wouldn't pay the bribes, French privateers attacked the American ships. As a result, America feared engaging France in a war. Adams, however, was instrumental in limiting that war, known as the Quasi-War, to naval engagements.

Despite Adams' successes, the opposing party—the Democratic-Republicans—predicted that John Adams would be a one-term president. That he was, but it was due to a number of unfavorable factors—most of which were unavoidable. First of all, he had to raise money for a national navy and a military force. This created unpopular taxation, but those fleets and forces became crucial in the years that followed. Adams also witnessed some of the most vicious political battles between the Federalists and the Democratic-Republicans during his presidency. However, Adams was tough and weathered through that crisis.

Despite some of the controversial policies that John Adams enacted, he was a president that guided the young country of the United

States to its feet. It is to his credit that he was able to maintain neutrality while Europe waged yet another war. With the country still in its nascent stages, the country would have floundered under such a heavy debt and perhaps would have never become what it is today.

Chapter 1 – John Adams: Political Activist

In 1735, John Adams was born in Braintree (currently Quincy), Massachusetts, in a small saltbox house, a style that was typical of the colonial era and characterized by its sloping roof. Ever since he was born, John Adams' father, John Sr., planned on his son becoming a Congregational minister like he was. Although young John was raised in a family that was dedicated to pursuing and upholding the beliefs of the church, he himself had no inclination to join the ministry. When he was a young student, he often played truant while attending Latin school, and his intense dislike of the headmaster there also discouraged him from taking any interest in becoming a minister. Adams felt that some preachers "pretended sanctity" and sounded like "absolute dunces" when they addressed their congregations. However, he did appreciate the values imparted through religion, and his later writings reflected his deep sense of spirituality.

Besides being a minister, John's father was also a farmer. The family leased their land in the beginning, but later, Deacon Adams bought a nine-acre lot which he later expanded into a 35-acre estate. The Adams' family had an active orchard, as the family was quite fond of apple cider, and grew vegetables—mostly staples like corn and potatoes. The family also owned some barnyard animals who would graze on the slopes of their land. Braintree was truly a beautiful area to settle down and raise a family in. It was situated in a river basin and was very fertile. There were meadows, woods, and streams, and the people themselves were very friendly as well. The people of Braintree leased land from each other, and in times of drought, the entire community shared their food with each other. About the family farm and its environs, young John Adams wrote, "I take great pleasure in viewing and examining the magnificent prospects that lie before us in this town."

But Adams wasn't content to live there forever, and in 1751, he entered Harvard University. Like many young men in his position, he wasn't sure what career path to take. These were tumultuous times for the thirteen colonies who were under the dominion of Great Britain. By the time John Adams graduated from Harvard, most of his peers had entered the military to make a living. John didn't choose to follow suit as he wanted to make his mark on history. He felt that he could make more of an impact as a lawyer than a soldier. To earn money for his tuition in law school, Adams taught school in Worcester and then studied law under John Putnam, a respected attorney in the community. In 1758, he was admitted to the bar. Although he was offered a job as a registrar of deeds, he turned it down and returned home, hoping to find a more exciting opportunity. Back in Braintree, Adams opened a small practice to help clients resolve local legal disputes.

While living once again in his hometown, John met a woman named Abigail Smith, who intrigued him. She was straightforward in her speech and never hesitated in carrying on debates with Adams about politics and social issues. His father was fond of Abigail, but his mother was hesitant since Abigail was the daughter of a humble farmer. After noting that he continued to court her, his mother accepted her, and he married Abigail in 1764. They lived on the farm he inherited from his father, who had died in 1761. John had once fancied that he might become a gentleman farmer, but the unrest in Boston, and indeed in all of the colonies, became a paramount concern.

John Adams and the Stamp Act

Times were changing in the thirteen colonies. The Seven Years' War (1756-1763) was mostly fought in Europe, but a portion of the war spilled over into North America. That segment was called the French and Indian War. Great Britain had instigated it as they wanted to expel the French from the North American mainland to increase their colonial holdings. After the war ended in 1763 with a British victory, Britain needed to find a way to pay off the debt incurred from the Seven Years' War, and they looked at the colonies as a way to both pay back their debts and reap a profit.

John Adams and his neighbors began to voice their extreme discontent with the monarchy and Parliament in England, who high-handedly rejected any objections the Massachusetts Bay Colony made in regard to the tax burden. The whole colony festered with unrest. To keep abreast of the events that affected Massachusetts, John often attended many of the town meetings in Boston, which was located nearby. At one such meeting, he met James Otis, a prominent leader of the city, who vigorously talked to the residents about the injustice of the newly-passed American Revenue Act, also known as the Sugar Act, of 1764, which actually lowered the tax on sugar. However, the colonists resented taxes that the English themselves didn't have to pay and viewed them as an infringement on their rights. At that meeting, Otis shot up and with great fury shouted, "Taxation without representation is tyranny!" Having been heavily influenced by the dynamism of Otis, John considered using his own knowledge of the law in the political arena.

To raise revenue for Great Britain, the British Parliament passed the Stamp Act of 1765. This act required that colonists pay for a special stamp that was placed on many papers carrying written material. When John Adams heard of this, he became incensed. Lawyers often need to use voluminous amounts of paper for their legal documents, and this directly affected his practice. In response to this crushing tax, Adams penned a series of articles under the pseudonyms, "Humphrey Ploughjogger," and "Mr. U." In the fall of the year 1765, he had them published in the *Boston Gazette*. It was an effort to make the reaction of an ordinary colonist to the Stamp Act known to the British authorities. In the letters, he warned their governor that colonists would resist these acts by refusing to buy the English products they regularly sold to the colonies.

> I do say, I won't buy one shilling's worth of anything that comes from old England, till the stamp act is repealed, nor I won't let any of my sons and daughters; I'd rather the Spittlefield weavers should pull down all the houses in old England, and knock the brains out of all the wicked great men there, than this country should lose their liberty. Our forefathers came over here for liberty of conscience, and we have been nothing better than servants to them all along this 100 years.

One of the more scholarly pieces he wrote was entitled *A Dissertation on the Canon and Feudal Law*, and it was published in the *London Chronicle*. Adams felt that an intellectual appeal to Great Britain might coax them into examining the colonial grievances more objectively. He used references from history and pointed out how the mindless application of feudal ideas create slaves and leave societies in ruins. John Adams' cousin, Samuel Adams, on the other hand, was belligerent about the unjust taxation and suppression. He favored violent protests as opposed to peaceful resistance. Samuel often met with his countrymen in the low light of dusk under a tall old elm tree in Boston—later dubbed the "Liberty Tree"—and suggested in engaging in more violent protests against the British officials stationed in Massachusetts. Samuel Adams' group called themselves the Sons of Liberty, and it was decided from the onset that they would operate in secret. Their singular goal was to undermine the high-handed rule of the colonial governors and the red-coated regiments that patrolled the cities and countryside. While they started out simply burning an effigy of Andrew Oliver, a local tax collector, mob violence broke out in various quarters of Boston. The Sons of Liberty were also instrumental in the destruction of the home of the English-appointed lieutenant governor of the colony, Thomas Hutchinson. John Adams eschewed these acts of vandalism and continued to urge the people of Massachusetts to engage in passive resistance. He rejected violence as the most appropriate means to deliver a message, and that remained a goal throughout his entire life. Although John did eventually join the Sons of Liberty, it was with the purpose of keeping abreast of events in Massachusetts, as he still preferred the use of reasoning and the law as a means to right a wrong. Others, like James Otis and Boston selectman John Hancock, recommended this as well.

The Commonwealth of Pennsylvania and some of the other colonies hired the statesman Benjamin Franklin to represent them directly in England and present a case for a reduction in taxes. Due to Franklin's efforts, the mounting pressure, and rise in violent protests in the colonies, the Stamp Act of 1765 was repealed in 1766.

Townshend Acts

During the years of 1765 through 1770, England's Cabinet was undergoing a troublesome turnover. William Pitt the Elder was one of the most capable parliamentarians in England. He had the uncanny ability to assess a need and propose a practical solution. After Pitt campaigned with the prior Prime Minister Lord Rockingham for the repeal of the Stamp Act, King George III burdened him with the duty of selecting new Cabinet members. Unfortunately, though, Pitt became ill. This created problems because he now couldn't monitor the performance of the new Cabinet members he selected.

Charles Townshend was one of the men Pitt appointed, and he accepted the role of Chancellor of the Exchequer. Townshend was an energetic man, and he was eager to please the king because he was politically ambitious. Therefore, he was determined to obtain revenue from the colonists but only managed to compound the problem. Between 1767 and 1768, he convinced Parliament to approve a number of revenue-raising mandates:

- *The New York Restraining Act of 1767*

This act obligated the colonists to house and support British soldiers as they had been doing since the French and Indian War. Because so many of these soldiers were quartered in New York, this act was specifically written for them.

- *The Revenue Act of 1767*

Townshend was a clever man, and he determined what products could not be manufactured in the colonies and would need to be purchased from Great Britain, which included items such as glass, painters' pigments, tea, and paper. A tax was placed on each of those items.

- *The Indemnity Act of 1767*

The colonies often bought tea smuggled into the country by the Dutch because it was less expensive than the British tea. To help the floundering British East India Company, the British permitted the company to sell directly to the colonies. The colonists still had to pay a tax, but it was less than they had been paying, and the British hoped that this would spread some goodwill. However, this act infuriated the colonies because it helped create an English monopoly on tea.

- *The Commissioners of Customs Act of 1767*

Customs on products shipped to the thirteen colonies were administered by British officials in England. Great Britain then established customs houses in the colonies. Most of them were housed in Boston, and the purpose of this act was to make sure that the laws were enforced better and that smuggling decreased.

- *The Vice-Admiralty Court Act of 1768*

This was an effort to curtail the smuggling of goods from other countries. Although penalties had regularly been levied for smuggling, the cases had been tried in colonial courts. This act required that smuggling cases be heard by a court appointed by the Royal Navy.

John Adams: Clever Counsel

In 1768, a case came up before the Vice-Admiralty Court in Massachusetts related to the newly passed Townshend Acts. John Adams demonstrated his peerless abilities as a defense lawyer in this case, which was brought against John Hancock, a well-known shipper in Boston. The case was a prime example of the misapplication of two of the Townshend Acts—the Customs Act and the Vice-Admiralty Act.

Because of the smuggling that occurred in the port of Boston, the British officials were on high alert. An English warship, the HMS *Romney*, was sent to Boston to stand by in order to eliminate the incidents of smuggling.

When Hancock's ship was docked, the British Board of Commissioners attempted to board it to inspect the cargo. However, they lacked the proper paperwork, so Hancock refused to permit the inspectors aboard. When they returned the next day with the appropriate warrants, he had his men unload the vessel, which included 25 kegs of wine. Hancock then paid the taxes on the alcohol to Thomas Kirk, the customs official. Once that was accomplished, Hancock went home. However, the British agents tallied at the dock and began to think that his shipment of wine had been very small. They suspected that more wine had been offloaded into smaller vessels before the *Liberty* docked. The commissioners weren't required to inspect the smaller ships as they could easily dock and unload cargo. They would have let the matter go, but Thomas Kirk then changed his story. He told the British agents that Captain Marshall of the *Liberty* locked him in the hold and threatened his life if he reported anything amiss. To make matters worse, Kirk went on to say that he heard the sounds of seamen unloading cargo while he was being confined. This revised statement was then reported to Comptroller Benjamin Hallowell who instructed Joseph Harrison, the Customs Collector, to seize the vessel. Harrison alerted the HMS *Romney* and asked them to assist. A few seamen at the dock suggested that Harrison notify John Hancock before taking action, but Harrison ignored their advice. Therefore, the HMS *Romney* attempted to seize the *Liberty*, and a fight broke out. Eventually, the sailors calmed themselves down and disembarked from Hancock's sloop. Then the *Liberty* was seized. A crowd had noted this commotion from the shore, which swelled to about 3,000 people. They tore through the port district searching for Hallowell and Harrison but couldn't find them. So, instead, the angry colonists broke all the windows in Hallowell's house and hauled Harrison's pleasure craft ashore. They dragged it to the Liberty Tree where they watched it burn. Riots erupted all over the city. This frightened not only Hallowell and Harrison but the entire Board of Commissioners who sought refuge aboard the HMS *Romney*.

According to the court records, Hancock was charged with failure to pay the duties on the wine reportedly unloaded from his ship. Hancock denied it and retained John Adams as the counsel for his defense. Court officials arrived from Great Britain for the trial, but the case was poorly handled by the British authorities.

It also didn't help the British authorities that Adams' legal mind was like a vise, and he seized upon the errors and inconsistencies in the conduct of the British court officials. First of all, they hadn't appointed judges within the deadline specified, so Adams tried to have a mistrial declared because of that. Adams' next targets were the witnesses called by the prosecution. Because of his two disparate affidavits, Kirk's testimony needed to be corroborated. Therefore, witnesses were needed. However, the customs official who was serving with Thomas Kirk admitted he was asleep during the incident and was unable to testify. To make matters worse for the Crown, their star witness, Joseph Maysel, was a man who had a history of perjury, so he was rejected as a credible witness, and his testimony was never heard. Captain Marshall was the captain of the schooner at the time so he could have been called as a witness; however, he died before the trial took place.

John Adams also didn't argue on the basis of whether there was or wasn't wine smuggled from the *Liberty* when it was at sea. He argued on the technical grounds that 1) the Vice-Admiralty Court hadn't chosen its judges in time for the trial and missed the proscribed deadline, 2) the death of Captain Marshall, 3) the testimony of Thomas Kirk couldn't be corroborated, and 4) Joseph Maysel couldn't be cross-examined having been discredited as a witness. Due to the embarrassment caused by the inept officials and the riots this case triggered, the newly formed Vice-Admiralty Court decided to drop all the charges!

Chapter 2 – From Counsel to Patriot

Tensions in the colonies continued to be high, especially due to the presence of increasing numbers of British soldiers in or near the port of Boston. Mobs of colonists flocked around the city. On one occasion, a crowd gathered around a store owned by a known Loyalist. They shouted and threw rocks, breaking a window in his house. A customs officer who lived nearby responded by firing shots. Tragically, he accidentally killed Christopher Seider, an eleven-year-old. Emotions were already at a fever pitch, and this only managed to outrage the colonists more. British soldiers were on high alert.

Defense Attorney for the British Soldiers: The Boston Massacre

Fistfights between colonists and soldiers were commonplace all over Boston after the *Liberty* affair. On March 5, 1770, a riotous crowd gathered in front of a customs house, and British soldiers under the command of Captain Thomas Preston rushed to the scene. A colonist threw an object, knocking one of the soldiers down. Shots rang out upon the crowded street. Preston hollered out an order to cease fire, which they did, but it was too late. Sixteen colonists lay bleeding upon the cobblestones; five of them died due to their injuries. More soldiers raced to the scene. In an effort to quell the rioting public,

Governor Thomas Hutchinson announced from the safety of town hall that Preston and his soldiers would be put on trial. The crowd then quieted down.

The Governor's Council scheduled the case for the end of October of that year and decided to hear the case at Castle William rather than Boston in an attempt to eliminate bias in the jury selection. In addition, there were no Bostonians on that jury.

There was some difficulty in naming an attorney for the defense, but as an honorable attorney, John Adams accepted the role of defense counsel. He believed that all people had the right to legal counsel regardless of their guilt, innocence, or public sentiment. In his defense, Adams carefully described the nature of the violence on the part of the colonists because they hit the soldiers' rifles with sticks and threw snowballs at them constantly. He indicated that it was a provocation on their end. In his closing statement, Adams said that a verdict should only be based on the facts of the case and not on the public sentiment toward Great Britain. He then quoted Algernon Sidney, an English parliamentarian, who said that the law "…is inexorable to the cries and lamentations of the prisoners…and deaf as an adder to the clamors of the populace." Two of the British soldiers were convicted, but the rest of the defendants, including Captain Preston, were acquitted. Today, Castle William is called Fort Independence.

After his experience defending the soldiers from the Boston Massacre, Adams felt that issues could still be resolved between the thirteen colonies and Great Britain, although it would take great effort. Adams' opinion changed considerably in the next two years, however, due to new, more repressive laws that applied to the thirteen colonies. These laws didn't apply to British citizens living in England, and since the citizens in the colonies viewed themselves as British citizens, they felt they were entitled to the same rights. Adams felt that the opinions that Great Britain had of the colonies had "undergone as many changes as the moon."

Transformation into Revolutionary

In 1772, the great statesman, Benjamin Franklin, was sent copies of thirteen letters sent from the governor of Massachusetts, Thomas Hutchinson, and the lieutenant governor, Andrew Oliver, to the British Parliament. These letters suggested that there should be a curtailment of the rights the Massachusetts colonists were originally entitled to as English subjects. Although Franklin didn't want the letters made public, John Adams felt that they should be. He said that Hutchinson had professed to be a defender of liberty, but his real sentiments were revealed in these letters. Adams had some of the content published in the *Boston Gazette*.

There were other changes afoot that affected the accountability of the governor and his top officials. The governors of Massachusetts had been paid for their services by the colonial legislature since the founding of the colony. The British government started paying the salaries of the colonial governors and judicial representatives in the colonies. This would shift the accountability of the provincial judges and representatives from the colonists to the Crown. During that crucial year, Governor Hutchinson gave a speech to the people of Massachusetts in which he insisted that the powers of the British Parliament over the colonies were absolute. The people were furious. In response, John Adams, Samuel Adams, and a lawyer and minister named Joseph Hawley III created a resolution that stated independence was a much better alternative than tyranny.

After the changes were made to the justice system as a result of the Vice-Admiralty Act of 1768, Hutchinson started applying its provisions by moving some of the trials from Massachusetts to England. This enraged the colonists. They couldn't afford to pay for colonial lawyers to travel to Britain and lodge there, and they also felt that the juries there would be biased.

The Boston Tea Party

Because the colonists had no representatives in the British Parliament, they viewed the Townshend Acts and the later Tea Act of 1773 as discriminatory and illegal. To protest their lack of representation in Britain, the citizens of Boston targeted the tea shipments, as it was the most popular drink in the colonies. In the winter of 1773, tea shipments arrived in Boston, but the people rejected it. Hutchinson responded by forbidding the ships to return to England with the tea, so they remained moored there in the harbor. John Adams wrote in his diary that accepting the tea would be tantamount to "giving up American posterity to ignominy, desolation and oppression and to poverty and servitude."

On December 16, 1773, the Sons of Liberty, some of whom were disguised as Native Americans, forcibly boarded the ships and dumped the tea overboard—over 92,000 pounds of it! This deliberative action was called the Boston Tea Party. John Adams said, "This destruction of the tea is so bold, so daring, so firm, intrepid and inflexible, and it must have important consequences, so lasting that I can't help but consider it an Epoch in History."

The British were vengeful. They felt that these colonists needed to be disciplined like naughty children, and their next move aimed to do just that.

The Coercive Acts

In 1774, Great Britain passed a series of punitive measures called the Coercive Acts. The passage of these laws wasn't as much of a legislative scolding as the Crown had hoped for. It was more of a provocation.

The Coercive Acts were called the Intolerable Acts by the colonists and consisted of the following:

> 1. *The Boston Port Act* – This closed the port of Boston until the destroyed tea had been paid for.
>
> 2. *The Massachusetts Government Act* – Town meetings in Boston were to be restricted, and the Governor's Council was no longer to be elected by the colonists; it was manned by

people appointed by the governor, who served directly under the government of Great Britain.

3. *The Administration of Justice Act* – This allowed for British soldiers and sailors charged for offenses under the Massachusetts legislation to receive a trial in Great Britain if the royal governor deemed that a fair trial in Massachusetts was not possible.

4. *The Quartering Act* – This applied to all colonists and allowed for the quartering of British soldiers in buildings owned by the colonists, which were to be made available upon demand

5. *The Quebec Act* – This act, although not related to the other acts when it was passed in the British Parliament, was still seen as one of the Intolerable Acts by the colonists. This enlarged the boundaries of the Province of Quebec and granted reforms that were very favorable to the Catholics living in the region.

The First Continental Congress

In the fall of 1774, the colonists decided to meet in secret in Philadelphia after the passing of the Intolerable Acts, and Adams was one of the individuals chosen to attend as a delegate for Massachusetts. Peyton Randolph, a wealthy planter from Virginia, was elected as the president of the Congress. Adams was very active in 1774 and met with all of the influential leaders in the colony at every meal, the tavern at night, and at the regularly scheduled meetings in Carpenter's Hall. The first issue discussed was the implication of the Intolerable Acts. He listened very carefully to what people said and recorded the comments he felt were crucial in framing a colonial reaction. Some of the delegates from Massachusetts were Samuel Adams; Thomas Cushing, a vociferous and popular lawyer and merchant; and Robert Treat Paine, a conservative who felt that reconciliation with Britain was still possible. Members of the First Continental Congress split along two lines: the conservatives and the rebels. For 22 grueling days, they argued. Adams spent a great deal of time trying to develop a compromise. Although some of the delegates felt it was futile, the Continental Congress decided to send a letter of grievances to King George.

One of the grievances on the list had to do with Massachusetts. In 1774, Thomas Gage replaced Hutchinson as governor. However, Gage was also the British general in charge of the colonies. The grievance stated: "The Commander-in-chief of all your Majesty's Forces in North America, had, in a time of peace, been appointed Governor of a colony." To the colonists, there seemed to be a conflict caused by serving in both capacities.

Among the other grievances were objections to the fact that the colonists had no representation in the British Parliament, the alteration of the justice system which had affected the impartiality of the judges, the many duties and taxes that were levied on the colonists, and the quartering of British troops on private property belonging to the colonists. As a lawyer, John Adams was particularly perturbed by the alterations in the justice department. Adams objected to the fact that the colonist's right to a trial by a jury of his own peers was now changed because of the Vice-Admiralty Court Act. A colonist could now be coerced into going to a court where Royal Navy officials would preside and no colonial peers would be allowed to participate in the jury.

The letter was overly polite and regularly punctuated with compliments for the fairness of the king. In parts, it begged for relief but confirmed loyalty to England by stating to the king, "Your royal authority over us and our connection with Great Britain we shall always carefully and zealously endeavor to support and maintain." One of the most conservative members of the First Continental Congress was Joseph Galloway, a lawyer from Pennsylvania. He was very critical of the letter of grievances. Galloway was against any revolutionary violence and was a self-admitted Loyalist. He did, however, prefer that legislature be established in the colonies similar to the House of Commons in England. To promote his opinion, Galloway presented a meticulously worded proposal to be sent to Great Britain. It was totally rejected. Disgusted by what he considered traitorous discussions, he stormed out before the meeting was adjourned. The man then impulsively joined General Howe's British regiment! Despite the fact that many colonists felt their rights were being infringed upon, there were still quite a few who remained loyal to the Crown, which often only furthered the tensions felt in the colonies.

In the middle of their discussions one day in September, the session was interrupted by the sudden arrival of Paul Revere. Rushing into the meeting room, Revere presented the Suffolk Resolves. They were composed by Dr. Joseph Warren, president of the provincial council of Massachusetts. The Suffolk Resolves proposed that the council continue to meet despite the fact that the governor had prohibited such meetings. In addition, the Suffolk Resolves asserted that Massachusetts should state its non-allegiance with the governor and end all trade with Great Britain. The Continental Congress endorsed these resolves. The delegates agreed that their respective colonies should participate in the embargo and encourage self-reliance so the colonies could manufacture what they need rather than depend upon shipments of British-made products.

As part of the agenda, it was recommended that the colonies set up their own militias and collect weapons and military equipment. Many, if not most, realized that war was inevitable and imminent.

Earlier in the sessions, Adams and the Continental Congress had received an inaccurate report delivered by a special messenger on September 6 that reported soldiers had fired on people in Boston. Patrick Henry was quick to respond, "The distinctions between Virginians, Pennsylvanians, New Yorkers and New Englanders are no more. I am not a Virginian, but an American." In actuality, the alleged incident was exaggerated because there was no shooting. As a precaution against any hostile actions, Governor Gage and his men started checking out some of the magazines and armories in the area.

They were observed by some of the colonists, and news of this search, later dubbed the Powder Alarm, raced around the colonies along with its inaccuracies. After hearing the report, the Sons of Liberty quickly formed a militia and marched toward Charlestown. When General Gage discovered that, he kept a cautious watch on Massachusetts. After the initial session of the Continental Congress was adjourned, Adams published a series of letters in the *Boston Gazette* under the pseudonym "Novangelus." In essence, these letters alerted colonists to not let the British remove their rights as citizens lest they become like the vassal states of Europe and incur hardships as a result.

After the Powder Alarm occurred, Massachusetts set up an alarm system by which local residents and colonial leaders would be notified if there was unusual activity on the part of the British soldiers in the colony, specifically if they left Boston where they were stationed. This system was extremely useful as it served as a way to alert the local militias to arm themselves and defend the colonists against any aggressive actions. Members of the group whose job it was to initiate the alarm were called Minutemen, and they were among the first to fight in the upcoming war.

Chapter 3 – The Second Continental Congress

The Conciliatory Resolution

In February of 1775, several influential members of King George's Cabinet attempted to avoid the pending war with the colonies with what was entitled the Conciliatory Resolution which would grant some of the colonists' demands. The original proposal was penned by William Pitt the Elder, who had been ill but briefly returned to his post as prime minister. He had a reputation for being more liberal in dealing with the colonies and proposed that more freedoms should be given to the colonies so they could rule themselves. Also, Pitt felt that some of the provisions of the Coercive Acts should be repealed. There were reportedly fierce arguments that followed the presentation of Pitt's proposal, so only a weakened version was passed and sent to the individual colonies. It indicated that the colonies who were willing to pay for the common defense and administer justice against those who resisted British authority in the colonies would be excused from paying some taxes but not those that would interfere with control of commerce.

The Battles of Lexington and Concord

As a result of the work of the First Continental Congress, the colonists began building up storehouses of arms. Many of these were on the private properties of the colonists since they knew the British were aware of the location of armories and weapons depots in the colonies. Boats came ashore at the Charles River toward Charlestown near the road to Lexington and Concord. The Minutemen that spotted them sent out an alert about Gage's activities, and at nightfall on April 18, 1775, one of the church officials hung two lanterns in the steeple of the Old North Church. The prearranged signal was that one lantern meant the British were arriving via a land route (which would have taken longer) and two lanterns meant they were coming by sea. Those two lanterns informed the colonists that the British were coming inland from the Charles River. Three Patriots, Paul Revere, William Dawes, and Samuel Prescott, rode through the local towns, spreading the word. Shortly after that, the colonial militia met with John Adams and John Hancock briefly at Lexington Common, which was south of the Charles River. Gage organized a unit of 700 British soldiers and gave them orders to search the colony of Massachusetts for weapons. The men concluded that Gage and the British redcoats were going to head for Concord where there was a weapons depot. All the weapons in it had already been hidden, but the British didn't know that. Since the British force was so large, the colonial militia dogged them. Several hundred townspeople also arrived. Major John Pitcairn, leading the British out of Lexington, saw the militia near a bridge and commanded them to disarm. The militia, under Colonel John Parker, didn't comply. A shot was fired; it is still unknown to this day which side shot first. The British then let loose a volley of shots. Eight members of the militia were killed, and ten men were wounded.

From there, the redcoats marched on to Concord in search of weapons. The colonial militia confronted them there also. Gunfire erupted, and 73 British soldiers were killed. The colonists lost 49 men, including one of their commanders, Isaac Davis. John Adams recorded in his diary, "The battle of Lexington, on the 19th of April, changed the instruments of warfare from the pen to the sword."

Adams rode to a local militia encampment at Cambridge (formerly Charlestown) and remarked that there was "great confusion and much distress." He also noted there wasn't enough artillery and provisions there. Following that visit, Adams rode the route where the battles had taken place, asking questions of the inhabitants. After those conversations, he was convinced that the colonies had reached the point of no return. The war had begun.

As he was preparing for his journey to Philadelphia for the Second Continental Congress, Adams realized that a revolutionary fever had infected everyone he met. By the time he reached Philadelphia, crowds of people had gathered around Adams and those he had traveled with on the way there.

On the Way to Independence

The Second Continental Congress assembled in 1775 and ran until 1781. The same delegates that collected in Philadelphia were the same as those at the First Continental Congress, along with some new delegates which included Thomas Jefferson, the young statesman from Virginia, as well as James Wilson, an accomplished lawyer, and Benjamin Franklin, a prolific writer and inventor, from Pennsylvania. Lyman Hall represented Georgia, the only colony without a delegate at the First Continental Congress. At the time, that colony was having a problem with a Native American rebellion and needed the support of British troops, so they had refrained from attending. John Hancock was another delegate sent from Massachusetts. Adams knew Hancock from when he had defended him on the charge regarding his shipping business. Peyton Randolph, an established attorney, was elected the president of the Congress again, but the very popular Hancock replaced him later on when Randolph was called back to Virginia by the governor.

The first item on the agenda was what came to be called the Olive Branch Petition. It was proposed and written by John Dickinson, the author of the *Letters from a Farmer in Pennsylvania* which were written in protest to the Townshend Acts. Unlike many of the other delegates, Dickinson felt that there was a clear distinction between Parliament and the king. Therefore, he felt that another petition should be sent directly to the king so he could redress the grievances of the colonies, which might result in reconciliation with Great Britain. A few others in the Congress supported the petition as well.

John Adams, however, rejected the Olive Branch Petition, and other delegates agreed with him. A debate followed. Adams stepped out of that assembly briefly, but Dickinson followed him into the yard and argued with him vehemently, saying "If you don't concur with us in our pacific system, I and a number of us will break off from you in New England, and we will carry on the opposition by ourselves in our own way." John Adams was angry and retorted, "I am not to be threatened into an express adoption or approbation of measures which my judgment reprobates." Adams and Dickinson never spoke to one another privately again during the meeting. Despite the protests against it, a sufficient number of delegates voted that the Olive Branch Petition be sent to the king, and so, it was.

The next item on the agenda had to do with making a declaratory statement related to the rights of the colonies to provide arms for their quickly forming militias. Although that task had already begun after the First Continental Congress, Benjamin Franklin felt that a workable procedure needed to be specified in writing. John Dickinson wrote the final draft, working upon the earlier draft written by Thomas Jefferson, called the Declaration of the Causes and Necessity of Taking Up Arms which was adopted in July of 1775.

The Conciliatory Resolution proposed by Britain had finally reached the Continental Congress and was discussed at length. John Rutledge, a lawyer from Charleston, South Carolina, asked the crucial question, "Do we aim at independence? Or do we only ask for restoration of rights and putting us on our old footing as subjects of the crown?" The Congress split into two factions over the matter. Even those who felt that a war might be necessary imagined that just the Battles of Lexington and Concord would be sufficient to convince Great Britain to put the colonies back on the same footing they were before the heavy taxation was imposed. In addition, there were London merchants who petitioned England to reconcile, so that trade could be normalized. Some of the merchants in Philadelphia and New York were in favor of reconciliation.

The opposition, however, felt that the resolution was "too little, too late," and they made an issue out of the fact that the colonies weren't even permitted to raise their own revenues to provide for themselves in terms of defense and justice. Throughout the summer of 1775, those in favor of reconciliation weakened. Realizing that they weren't even going to be funded for curtailing raids from Native Americans and had little by way of supplies for border protection, the colonists drew up regulations to guide the state militias plans for a rudimentary navy and took over foreign policy.

John Adams then stood up in the assembly, stressing that this was an issue that required patience. He said, "We must suffer people to take their own way" although path they take may not be the "speediest and surest." The Congress took fourteen months to discuss the Conciliatory Resolution, but also remembered the words of King George III who said that the hostilities in the colonies formed a "wicked and desperate conspiracy." Suggestions arose in Congress about the creation of an army. James Wilson of Pennsylvania objected. However, despite that Congress rejected his opinion about making yet another overture of peace. In the heat of the moment, Samuel Adams leaped up and called those who supported reconciliation the "tools of a tyrant."

John Adams then boldly proposed that the Congress appoint a general. Adams felt that there was one member of the Congress well suited for that role, and that man was George Washington. A large militia unit was already in Charlestown, Adams added, and an army could start with them. The assembly concurred, and Washington became the commander-in-chief of the Continental Army. Washington was ready for the challenge, so he immediately left the Congress in order to recruit troops.

In the summer of 1775, Richard Penn, the lieutenant governor of Pennsylvania, and Arthur Lee brought a copy of the Olive Branch Petition to Lord Dartmouth, the British representative in the colonies and asked for a response. Dartmouth forwarded it to England and reported back a month later, "We were told that as his Majesty did not receive it on the throne, no answer will be given." However, this is not what happened. The British already knew its contents because they intercepted a packet of letters aboard a ship. One of the items in the packet was a private letter from John Adams to a friend that showed he wasn't in favor of the petition. The British were aware that John Adams was an influential leader among the colonists, and the British realized that there wasn't a consensus among the people. The Olive Branch Petition also reached England around the time of the Battle of Bunker Hill, so it became a moot point anyway.

The Battle of Bunker Hill

While the Second Continental Congress was in session, colonial militiamen heard a rumor that the British planned on fortifying the hills around Boston. To prevent British infiltration into the colony, Colonel William Prescott sent in his men to occupy those positions under cover of darkness. On the morning of June 17, 1775, the British, under the command of General William Howe, attacked them. Even though the colonists had the advantage of higher ground, they lost the battle because their ammunition ran out. Despite their victory, the British incurred a lot of casualties.

Following that, King George III issued the Proclamation of Rebellion. It stated that portions of the colonies were in "open and avowed rebellion" against Great Britain. Even though the American supporters in England told their monarch that the actions of the

British were driving the colonies toward declaring independence, he persisted in getting the proclamation passed.

Two months later, Great Britain passed the Prohibitory Act, which essentially closed all of the ports of the colonies to foreign trade. When that act was passed, the Continental Congress sent the Connecticut merchant, Silas Deane, on a secret mission to France to secure weapons and assistance in furthering their cause. Deane secured heavy weapons along with the help of the famous Major General the Marquis de Lafayette. Deane was also instrumental in smuggling badly needed goods to the colonies during the closure of Boston Harbor. Some of those supplies arrived in North Carolina and were shipped north, and more were brought to the Continental troops with Lafayette's assistance.

The Lee Resolution

In 1776, Richard Henry Lee made a motion, recommending that a resolution be passed declaring independence of the colonies. That body would, he said, "best conduce to the happiness and safety of their constituents in particular, and America in general." John Adams seconded that motion. This resolution was carefully reworded and called the Lee Resolution. The proposal was approved in May of that year, and the stage was set for the writing of the Declaration of Independence. Three committees were appointed to develop the wording of the resolution, and Adams himself served on two of the three committees.

The final resolution, completed in July of 1776, stated:

> Resolved, that these United Colonies are, and right ought to be, free and independent States, that they are absolved from all allegiance to the British Crown, and that all political connection between them and the State of Great Britain is, and ought to be, totally dissolved.
>
> That it is expedient forthwith to take the most effectual measures for forming foreign Alliances.

That a plan of confederation be prepared and transmitted to the respective Colonies for their consideration and approbation.

The Declaration of Independence

One of the committees that arose from the Lee Resolution was known as the Committee of Five. They were tasked with the job of drafting a statement that declared the colonies' independence to the world. The Committee consisted of John Adams, Thomas Jefferson, Benjamin Franklin, Roger Sherman of Connecticut, and Robert Livingston from New York.

After outlining the general principles of freedom, many of which were inspired by Thomas Paine, an English statesman, and discussing its content, Jefferson suggested that John Adams write the initial draft of the Declaration of Independence to present to the Second Continental Congress to vote upon. He declined Jefferson's recommendation, saying:

> Reason first: You are a Virginian and a Virginian ought to appear at the head of this business. Reason second: I am obnoxious, suspected and unpopular. You are very much otherwise. Reason third: You can write ten times better than I can.

Virginia was generally recognized as the wealthiest of the thirteen colonies so having their approval was of the utmost importance. John Adams was also a forceful man who recognized his own limitations, one of them being a tendency to be abrasive at times. Thomas Jefferson was noted as a prolific writer and had received many accolades for the quality of his writing. Therefore, the Committee approved of Thomas Jefferson to write the first draft of the declaration.

As per his reputation for speed, Thomas Jefferson produced the Declaration of Independence in 17 days. Other members of Congress made some changes, and it was then sent out to all the colonies for ratification.

While the Declaration of Independence was circulating throughout the colonies, more British warships were arriving in the port of New York. George Washington scrambled to set up fortifications on the western end of Long Island in the area currently known as Brooklyn, but Manhattan Island itself was poorly defended. The colonial troops were fresh and inexperienced because Washington didn't have sufficient resources to train them. Not only that, but some of the new recruits were insubordinate, and some quit when Washington initiated a program of discipline. The Continental Congress recognized this and appointed Adams as the administrator of the Board of War and Ordinance. Adams realized that soldiers should be paid for their services and that they needed an incentive to fight in addition to patriotism. Therefore, as his first act, Adams had the Continental Congress pass resolutions providing salaries and a grant of land for the men if they remained in military service. In addition, he had regulations passed regarding discipline and set up a special committee to arrange for provisions and supplies.

On July 4, 1776, the Declaration of Independence was passed. But because the War for Independence was happening faster than military preparations were progressing, New York fell to the British. General William Howe, who replaced Thomas Gage as the head of the British army in the colonies, attempted to put the war to an end and called upon the colonies to send representatives to Staten Island for a conference. John Adams, Benjamin Franklin, and Benjamin Rush, a physician from Philadelphia, met with him. Howe tried to assuage the group by saying that he viewed them as legitimate British subjects. To that, Adams replied, "Your Lordship may consider me in what light you please, except for that of a British subject." After fruitless discussions with Howe, the delegation realized that General Howe had no authority to formulate a treaty anyway, and they promptly left.

The Articles of Confederation

In 1776, at one of the sessions of the Continental Congress, the colonists realized that they were acting in the capacity of a government that was separate from that of British America. The Continental Congress appointed John Dickinson to head a committee whose purpose was to draw up a united plan for a government that had representation from each of the colonies. The Congress then contacted the colonies and informed them to set up local governments of their own and write their own constitutions. After that happened, the Congress proposed that the colonies call themselves "states." This conversion of the term from "colony" to "state" had to be ratified by each colony, and it wasn't until 1790 that the entire process was actually completed.

Expenses related to the funding of a united government was also an issue. The Continental Congress finally decided that the financial obligations of each state would be determined upon the relative physical size of each state.

The tools and procedures for functioning as a representative government also needed to be clarified. The Congress drew up a series of thirteen articles, called the Articles of Confederation, to which each state would adhere. Amendments could be added to those articles via a voting procedure which required that at least two-thirds of the states approve them. The Articles of Confederation, after much debate, was passed in 1781.

This finalized structure was commendable, but some glaring factors were overlooked. Although there was a voting procedure in place, there was no consistent system enacted to levy and collect taxes, regulate trade, and conduct commerce, no set policy for conducting foreign affairs, no standard monetary policy, no national army or navy, and no judicial system for enforcing laws. In addition, no one particular person or persons were in charge of the new country, and there was no staff to support them.

The weaknesses of the Articles of Confederation became a stumbling block for John Adams in the years to come when he was called upon to function as a diplomat.

Chapter 4 – John Adams: Diplomat & Constitutionalist

As the administrator of the Board of War and Ordinance, Adams knew that the states weren't likely to win the Revolutionary War without the assistance of other nations. He presented this dilemma to the delegates of the Continental Congress, and they agreed. To attract the support of France in the war effort, Adams presented the idea that a favorable trade agreement might arouse their interest. At that point, though, the war wasn't going well, so France would have been unlikely to respond to a direct request for military assistance.

It was a known fact that Benjamin Franklin was popular in France due to the intense interest of the French in many of his innovative inventions. They also enjoyed him personally. Therefore, the Congress sent him there as a goodwill ambassador with the hopes that he might be able to convince France to offer military assistance. Having heard about the colonists' desire for independence from Silas Deane who consulted with him the year before, Lafayette was enthusiastic about helping out and went to America unofficially in 1777. When he was introduced to George Washington, they related to each other so well that they became lifelong friends. Due to Franklin's endeavors, a very skilled Prussian lieutenant, Baron von Steuben, who was in France on business, also expressed an interest, so he traveled to America to help as well. One of von Steuben's greatest strengths was his ability to train new recruits. He did that at Valley Forge, Pennsylvania, where the Continental Army was encamped for the winter. The colonial soldiers loved him as he was very humorous and witty. In later years, John Adams' son, Charles, lived with von Steuben for a time. It was rumored that they were homosexuals.

John Adams: Commissioner to France

Back in the states, the Continental Congress was growing impatient. Franklin was already over in France, but there was no commitment yet on their part. So, in November of 1777, they appointed John Adams as a commissioner to France to obtain an agreement. Arthur Lee, who had written some intense essays against the Townshend Acts, was also sent there as an aide in the negotiations. The journey across the Atlantic was hazardous, and they arrived later than they expected. Shortly after they had arrived, Adams and Lee conferred with Franklin to develop a treaty. Adams himself wrote the original draft. The French foreign minister, the Comte de Vergennes, signed the Treaty of Alliance and Treaty of Amity and Commerce but only after hearing about the Continental victory at the Battle of Saratoga in 1777. After that battle, France finally felt that the colonists' resolve was strong and that they might have the ability to win against France's perennial enemy, England.

Adams and Lee then met with Franklin to make some changes to the treaty to have them approved. The three commissioners had many differences among themselves, though. Adams felt that Franklin came across as too loyal to the French and seemed to be too old for the job. Lee, on the other hand, disliked Franklin intently and refused to cooperate, so he was sent to Spain to attempt to get their help. Adams, however, endeavored to create a working relationship with Franklin. Adams was concerned that France had yet to take any action to aid the states and contacted de Vergennes in that regard. However, Adams was unaware that de Vergennes was also focusing on the newly declared war between Britain and France over control of the West Indies when he suggested that France send over a naval fleet. De Vergennes was incensed about what he considered to be Adams' impertinence. He also disliked Adams because he spoke French very poorly. During the course of their negotiations, Adams admitted to de Vergennes that the value of their dollar had dropped. De Vergennes insisted that Adams write to the Continental Congress to get them to restore the dollar to its original value when trading with France under the treaty. That would, of course, cause a delay in the negotiations, but it was more of a tactic by de Vergennes to get rid of Adams for a while.

Adams still voiced his frustrations at the lack of progress on France's behalf though. The treaty with France had been made two years prior, and while France had dispatched Jean-Baptiste Donatien de Vimeur, better known as simply the Comte de Rochambeau, to assist George Washington in 1780, France had yet to do anything of significance. While Adams furiously wrote letters about this, de Vergennes wrote his own to the Continental Congress and informed them that he would only work with Franklin, and he later informed Adams of the same. Adams' diplomatic mission was the result of mishandled efforts on the part of an immature nation not yet familiar with dealing with foreign powers and who was also not careful enough to keep all channels of communication open.

Ambassador to the Dutch Republic

In 1780, John Adams went to the Dutch Republic. He didn't initially go in an official capacity, but he was later assigned the role of ambassador to the States-General, the administrative body of Holland. Adams knew that America desperately needed a loan, not only to help finance the war but to pay off their war debt. He sent numerous letters to the Dutch government, but there was no response, and many of the banks that Adams approached were reluctant to meet with him. One of the reasons for this was the fact that Holland hadn't yet recognized the right of America to achieve independence from Great Britain. The Dutch also depended heavily upon England for trade and wanted to remain neutral in the

American War of Independence. Interestingly, the Dutch proposal of neutrality angered the British and drove them to declare war on Holland at the end of 1780. During the following year of 1781, the British Lieutenant General Charles Cornwallis surrendered to George Washington at Yorktown, Virginia, and the American War of Independence was over.

In April of 1782, Adams finally received a response from the Dutch government and met with Prince William V of Orange. Holland finally recognized American independence in exchange for a Treaty of Amity and Commerce between America and their own country. In October of 1782, Adams made a proposal to that effect, and Dutch officials signed it after making a few changes. Adams then proudly stated in a letter to Robert Livingston,

> Upon the whole, I think the Treaty is conformable to the principles of perfect reciprocity, and contains nothing that can possibly be hurtful to America, or offensive to our allies, or to any other nation, except Great Britain, to whom it is indeed, without a speedy peace, a mortal blow.

Once the Dutch treaty was signed, Adams met with Joan van der Capellen, a Dutch nobleman who was a champion for the American cause. He had met der Capellen earlier, but the financier wasn't willing to commit any funds without his government's acknowledgment of American independence. To further aid John Adams, der Capellen introduced him to some bankers and advocated a loan for America. Due to van der Capellen's intercession and the new treaty, two very prominent bankers came forward to help America's cause—Nicolaas van Staphorst and Wilhelm Willink. When Adams returned to America, he had a guaranteed loan of two million dollars.

The Yorktown Campaign: End of the American Revolution

Before Adams made progress with the Dutch though, the war had already come to an end. In 1781, the American Revolution involved the land forces commanded by George Washington, the Comte de

Rochambeau, and the Marquis de Lafayette. These troops marched the entire length of the United States from Pennsylvania and Delaware all the way to Virginia. Naval forces paralleled them at sea in the Atlantic and were led by French fleets under François Joseph Paul, the Comte de Grasse, and Jacques-Melchior Saint-Laurent, known as the Comte de Barras, of the French Navy. The American land forces and the French naval forces combined were massive. The British land forces were heavily outnumbered, and they only had a small number of warships—about 63—and those were reportedly small.

Lieutenant General Charles Cornwallis had been the general in charge of the British forces in the south. In 1780, he was defeated at the Battle of Kings Mountain in South Carolina and again failed at the Battle of Cowpens, also in South Carolina, in 1781. He was promised reinforcements by General Henry Clinton, who was in Philadelphia. However, those reinforcements were delayed and didn't leave the harbor until a month later. In the meantime, Cornwallis sent out a message to Clinton, saying, "If you cannot relieve me very soon, you must prepare to hear the worst." The Continental Army and the French Navy soon after began a siege on the city of Yorktown, Virginia, on September 28. Although Cornwallis attempted to escape via the nearby waterways at Gloucester, he was unsuccessful. On October 19, 1781, he surrendered. He then sent General Clinton a letter stating:

> Sir, I have the mortification to inform your Excellency that I have been forced to give up the posts of York and Gloucester, and to surrender the troops under my command, by capitulation on the 19th instant, as prisoners of war to the combined forces of America and France.

Negotiator: Treaty of Paris

In 1782, Adams was appointed as one of the American Peace Commissioners to help formulate the terms of the Treaty of Paris, which officially ended the American War of Independence.

Benjamin Franklin, Thomas Jefferson (although he did not go to Europe like the other commissioners), Henry Laurens, and John Jay were tasked with working with Adams to negotiate with British, French, and Dutch officials.

John Adams had his 16-year-old son, John Quincy Adams, the future president of the United States, and his 13-year-old son, Charles, accompany him to France. John Quincy acted as his secretary, and Charles attended school in both France and the Netherlands. Both of his sons learned a number of languages while there.

While in Europe, Adams worked alongside a number of men to finalize the Treaty of Paris, and each brought along their own distinct advantages. Benjamin Franklin, the publisher and printer, had extensive experience in dealing with the British as well as the French. The British knew he was a clever inventor and scientist, and he had also been an agent for American commercial interests in the past. The officials of Great Britain treated him well because he was a very powerful representative of America. Henry Laurens was a merchant and a rice planter from South Carolina. He had experience working in the Netherlands and also had a good business relationship with Richard Oswald, one of the British officials assigned to help negotiate the treaty on behalf of England.

John Jay, a former president of the Continental Congress and a lawyer, was also sent because his sharp mind and sense of objectivity would help iron out any disagreements among the parties who would be discussing the terms.

Representing England was Richard Oswald and David Hartley. Oswald was a trader and had a good relationship with Ben Franklin, who once said of him that he was a man with an "air of great simplicity and honesty." Hartley was a respected member of Parliament, and he had positive relationships with Benjamin Franklin and Lord Rockingham, the prior prime minister of Great Britain. The British prime minister during these negotiations was

Lord Shelburne, a man whose history showed that he was understanding of the rights of Americans.

The French, led by the French Foreign Minister Vergennes, proved to be difficult to deal with over issues related to fishing rights in Newfoundland, Tobago Island, and Gibraltar. In fact, these disagreements stalled the formulation of the treaty. Most of the arguments stemmed from the fact that France, in their competition with England, wanted more restrictive measures than was deemed necessary. Therefore, John Adams and John Jay overruled Franklin's pro-French stance and decided to negotiate with Great Britain directly. Jay, Laurens, and Adams preferred that all parties make separate pacts with France regarding commercial interests. Franklin was an agreeable and humble man, so he gave them the leeway they requested.

There were ten points cited in the treaty with Great Britain:

> 1. Britain would acknowledge the independence of British America to be a free and sovereign country called the United States of America.
>
> 2. The boundaries of America would include the thirteen states and all the land over to the Mississippi River.
>
> 3. The United States would be granted fishing rights off Newfoundland and in the Gulf of Saint Lawrence.
>
> 4. Debts would be paid to the creditors on either side.
>
> 5. Americans would make restitution on confiscated lands belonging to British subjects that were seized during the war.
>
> 6. In the future, America would refrain from confiscating any land belonging to a British subject.
>
> 7. Prisoners of war would be released, except for British slaves who were still in America.
>
> 8. America and Great Britain would each have access to the Mississippi River.

9. Territories captured after this treaty would be returned without compensation.

10. Ratification would occur within six months.

The Treaty of Paris was signed on September 3, 1783, officially ending the war. It was a part of the set of agreements between the United States, Great Britain, France, Spain, and the Dutch Republic known as the Peace of Paris.

France also signed what was called the Treaties of Versailles of 1783. It granted France fishing rights in the west coast of Newfoundland and the Gulf of Saint Lawrence. The other points in this mutual treaty related to the possession of various islands in the Atlantic Ocean and near Europe and India.

The Dutch Republic participated in the peace process as well with their own treaty. They had a good relationship with France and worked with them so that they could regain the possession of their territories in the East Indies and the small country of Cape Apollonia in Africa that had been annexed by Great Britain. There was also a guarantee that there would be no British interference with oceanic traffic.

Spain gave up control of Florida to the British in exchange for Cuba. In addition, they received possession of French territories west of the Mississippi along with the Port of New Orleans.

Ambassador to England

Now that America was an independent country, it was vital to appoint ambassadors to represent their interests in foreign counties. In 1785, John Adams was appointed as the first American ambassador to Great Britain. His wife, Abigail, accompanied him there, and his son, John Quincy Adams, who was serving an American diplomat in Russia, came over to join his father as well. John Adams' rather challenging task was to warm up the relations with England following the revolution in order to reestablish trade between the two countries. Although Adams was successful in his relationship with King George III, the king had some reservations due to Adams' rocky relationship with France.

Adams had difficulties with some of the officials and courtiers in England. Before the war, Adams was a good friend of Jonathan Sewall while he was serving as the British attorney general of Massachusetts. During John Adams' ambassadorship, Sewall served as an attorney for King George. However, Sewall had a falling out with Adams due to their differences over the war and Adams' lack of social graces. Sewall said of Adams that "His abilities are undoubtedly equal to the mechanical parts of his business as ambassador, but this is not enough…he has none of those essential arts or ornaments which constitute a courtier." Sewall also added that he felt Adams was "quite out of his element." He had difficulty in blending pleasure with business, as the English were wont to do. Adams tended to ruminate and worry about the fulfillment of his duties as ambassador, and one of those concerns revolved around the payment of war debts.

According to Article 4 of the Treaty of Paris, Americans were expected to pay their debts back to English creditors. However, not all of these debts were repaid. In retaliation, some British soldiers still remained on American territory at forts that they had constructed prior to and during the revolution. Although Adams made a concerted effort to resolve those issues, there was no response from Congress, and he felt unsuccessful and frustrated. One of the reasons for the failure to collect monies to pay debts stemmed from a weakness in the Articles of Confederation. The Articles failed to provide for the enforcement of its precepts, causing John to reach a stalemate in that regard.

Shay's Rebellion

After the War of Independence, Adams' state of Massachusetts was inflicted with a cash shortage because foreign and state merchants began demanding that payments be made in hard currency. Prior to this, the merchants were satisfied with payment made in goods.

In 1786, a rebellion broke out highlighting four unresolved issues: failure to pay the salaries of Revolutionary War veterans, the high taxes the state of Massachusetts levied, the lack of value in the Continental dollar, and the confiscation of farm property from those who were unable to pay with hard currency. Hence, the courts were bombarded with petitions and complaints from mostly the merchants and war veterans. When the militia was called out, violent protests in the streets and towns continued. James Warren, who headed up the militia, wrote to Adams saying that "We are now in a state of anarchy and confusion bordering on civil war." Adams was extremely concerned and anxious about the situation; he was afraid that the United States might collapse while it was still in its nascent stages. He even suggested that these rebels should be executed. About a year later, the insurrection was stopped, and its leaders fled to other states. There was some loss of life during this rebellion, but Shay's Rebellion brought about a strong motive to correct the situation on a national level.

Constitutional Convention

Therefore, the Philadelphia Convention, better known now as the Constitutional Convention, was called into session in September of 1787. George Washington was unanimously elected as president of the convention. The assembly then decided to write a new constitution for the country because the Articles of Confederation had proven to be ineffective. John Adams didn't attend this convention as he was still serving in England, and neither did Thomas Jefferson, who was in France in a similar capacity.

The Articles of Confederation had deleteriously affected John Adams' performance, and some of the Founding Fathers discussed the problems flowing from these Articles and determined that the weaknesses were:

>1. The national government had no power to impose taxes as it only relied upon the willingness of states to contribute if a need was presented. If the states failed to remit payments,

there was no way to compel them to do so. Therefore, the country was underfunded and unable to pay its war debt.

2. The government had no power to impose duties or tariffs on foreign imports or to regulate interstate commerce as well as international commerce. As a result, American ports were flooded with goods, and the growth of American manufacturing was stunted by the competition.

3. There was no standardized currency, and the Continental dollar used during the war was worthless.

4. While various states may have had militias, there was no army or navy to protect the entire country, no system for recruiting people to join the armed forces, and no means to pay them.

5. There was no tool created to enforce the legislation that was included in the Articles of Confederation passed by the Continental Congress.

6. Although the Treaty of Paris allowed free access to the Mississippi River, there was no means to prevent a country from breaching that agreement.

7. Very often, the passage of new laws was often deadlocked when the Congress failed to produce a 2/3 majority on a vote.

8. The national government wasn't empowered to make treaties.

9. The voting system, which was based upon the size of a state, created a lopsided majority in favor of the Southern states. Therefore, the Northern states had no say in the measures that were passed.

While the issues of the Articles of Confederation were being nailed down and the United States Constitution was being created, Adams was becoming increasingly frustrated with his lack of progress. John Jay was the secretary for foreign affairs at the time. Because Adams was having enormous difficulties with his post in Britain, he asked Jay to be relieved. Jay politely assented, so Adams and Abigail returned to Massachusetts.

"Old Peacefield"

The purchase of a delightful farm and home called Peacefield while Adams was still in England served to take the sting out of a disappointing stint as the British ambassador. Of it, he said, "Improving my garden has more charms for my fancy than residing at the Court of Saint James." The farmhouse had been built in 1731, so it needed work, of course, but it had the makings of a lovely garden. There was an orchard on the property which was overgrown but still thriving. Abigail was excited and brought two cuttings with her from England—a white and a red rose bush. The roses represented the 16th-century insignias of the House of York (the white rose) and the House of Lancaster (the red rose). She also planted lilacs at the entryway. Those lilac bushes are actually still there today, now tended by the National Park Service.

Chapter 5 – John Adams: Vice President and Then President under the New Constitution

The Philadelphia Convention was attended by 55 of the 75 state delegates. They determined that they had to develop an effective organization that would resolve the weaknesses in the Articles of Confederation and that would establish a national government to lead all the states. After voting on plans submitted by several states, they decided upon establishing three branches of government: the executive, legislative, and judiciary branches, branches which are still used today in the United States.

The executive branch is made of a president, vice president, the Cabinet, and various departments and agencies. The president is the head of state and the government, the commander-in-chief, and the chief diplomat with the duty to name an attorney general and a postmaster general. The president can sign treaties and pass or veto legislation proposed by the legislative branch. The vice president is the presiding officer of the Senate (a part of the legislative branch) and takes the place of the president if he cannot fulfill the duties of his office, for example, due to death, illness, resignation, or removal. In 1789, the executive branch had two departments at the time: Foreign Affairs (later renamed State Department), to handle commerce, treaties, and international relations, and the Treasury Department to levy, collect, and distribute taxes according to the formulas laid out by Congress.

The legislative branch consists of a Senate and a House of Representatives, collectively known together as Congress. Prior to the establishment of the Constitution, the number of state representatives was determined based on the size of the state. However, that created bias. To resolve that, the Convention decided to have two senators per state, and the number of representatives in the House for a state depended upon the population of it. The function of the legislative branch is to pass laws.

The judicial branch was also created, separating the states into judicial districts. A US Supreme Court was also set up under Article III of the Constitution. The framework for the lower courts was created by the first Congress in the Judiciary Act of 1789 after the first president was elected. In the beginning, the president appointed the justices to the Supreme Court. Later on, those justices were subject to the approval of the Senate. The Supreme Court justices were also initially assigned to particular districts and traveled there to hear cases, much like circuit courts. In time, that was changed, and the Supreme Court now sits in Washington, DC. Their function, still to this day, is to enforce the laws of the land.

The first US Constitution was created in 1787. It had seven articles, eleven amendments, and the Bill of Rights, which contained ten items. One of the original 11 amendments wasn't ratified—one that would have required each district to not exceed a population of 50,000. More amendments were passed in later years, and today, there are 27 amendments in all.

James Madison and Alexander Hamilton contributed a great deal of the writing to the US Constitution. Nine states ratified the document on June 21, 1788, the required minimum needed to pass; however, the Constitution didn't go into effect until March 4, 1789. The

Constitution was eventually ratified by all the states, although this didn't happen until 1790.

When John Adams served as ambassador to Great Britain, he could have particularly benefited from the improved Constitution, especially Article I which would have given him the money to pay off foreign debt (from the Treasury), the power to take action against those who had failed to pay their debt (through the judicial department), and the ability to intercede with issues related to international commerce (through the state department).

Presidential Campaign

According to the US Constitution at that time, the president of America was elected by the majority of votes from the electors of each state. Whoever came in second in the count was appointed as vice president. For the 1789 election—the first one in the new nation of America—it was expected that George Washington would be elected. John Adams was also very popular and was a serious contender for the presidency as well. After the ballots were counted, Adams received 34 electoral votes and Washington got 69. Although he wasn't surprised that Washington won, Adams was upset that Washington received twice as many votes as himself. However, unbeknownst to him, Alexander Hamilton had written letters to some of the electors disparaging Adams. In one of them, he said:

> He is a man of an imagination sublimated and eccentric; propitious neither to the regular display of sound judgement, nor to steady perseverance in a systematic plan of conduct; and I began to perceive what has been since too manifest, that to this defect are added the unfortunate foibles of a vanity without bounds, and a jealousy capable of discoloring every object.

In addition to other criticisms, Hamilton contended that a person in high office should seek the advice of his advisors and others well respected in the areas of political philosophy. He also suggested that

John Adams would be too arrogant to seek advice from capable and reliable sources.

John Adams – Vice President

Having come in second, John Adams became the vice president. As vice president, he presided over the Senate. The very first debate Congress had was a curious one—what title should be given to the president and vice president, and how should they be addressed? Adams had a reputation for being rather aristocratic and suggested that the government of the United States wouldn't command respect around the world unless its chief executive had a "superior title." Adams especially liked the suggestion made by Representative George Tucker of South Carolina: "His Highness the President, Protector of the Liberties of the United States." Thomas Jefferson felt that particular title was "superlatively ridiculous." Adams' preference for extraordinary titles made him the subject of laughter and ridicule, and some people even jokingly called Adams "His Rotundity," a reference to his rather ample waistline. It was decided that the president would simply be called "Mr. President."

Adams also felt that he, as vice president, should live in an impressive home. So, he and his wife moved into the Richmond Hill mansion in New York, which was the first national capital under the Constitution.

Later on, during the second session of the US Congress, the Residence Act was passed, establishing the location of a national capital. Washington, DC, situated inside the borders of Maryland and Virginia, was envisioned as the central location of the original states. Those two states donated land for the creation of the capital, and funding was approved to erect majestic buildings for the use of federal officials and their staffs.

Despite the progress the nation was making in establishing itself, John Adams was unhappy with his role as vice president, serving two terms under George Washington. However, it might be said that he contributed to his own displeasure. Hamilton's comment that

Adams wasn't one to seek advice might have been well founded as Adams seemed to feel that the president should seek his advice instead of the reverse. He also felt the vice presidency role was an "inactive" one. In his personal papers, he sarcastically wrote: "My country in its wisdom contrived for me the most insignificant office that ever the invention of man or his imagination contrived or his imagination conceived." He also cynically remarked that "Franklin electrified (George Washington) with his rod – and henceforth these two conducted all the policy, negotiations, legislatures and war." However, it is worthy to note that Adams rarely attended Cabinet meetings, thus limiting himself.

Election of 1796: President John Adams

John Adams associated himself with the Federalist Party, which was also called the Pro-Administration Party. The Federalists espoused the concept of a strong central government and were basically conservative and pro-business. During Washington's term, the First Bank of the United States was established to provide for the stabilization of the fiscal policy and empower the government to pay debts and charge excise taxes and tariffs. Most of the Federalists lived in the northern states where manufacturing and business were prime occupations. In terms of trade, they preferred to deal with Great Britain, and the John Jay Treaty, negotiated in 1794, named Great Britain as their most favored trading partner.

The Democratic-Republican Party, created by Thomas Jefferson and James Madison, stood for the principle that states' rights were more important and that a highly centralized national government would be deleterious for the common man. In terms of trade, the Democratic-Republicans favored France over Britain. And as for the national bank, they were dead set against that, imagining that greedy Northerners would take undue advantage of farmers from rural America in the southern states.

Adams ran for the presidency in 1796 as a Federalist against Thomas Pinckney, also a Federalist. The Democratic-Republicans ran

Thomas Jefferson and Aaron Burr. Jefferson was extremely popular and favored as the top contender. However, the Democratic-Republican predilection for France made voters hesitate to vote for him as France was in the throes of the French Revolution, a violent grassroots movement that rocked the country and shook the entirety of Europe.

John Adams had strong opinions against the newly established French Republic because he felt that it was a form of unicameral legislation—that is, controlled by one political body without input from the opposition—and that there would be nothing "to restrain them from making tyrannical laws." In 1790 and 1791, he had anonymously published the *Discourses on Davila* in the *Gazette of the United States*, a Federalist publication. Davila was a 17th-century writer who wrote about the French wars of religion of that era. Adams' essay was originally meant as a translation, but he transformed it into a political commentary supporting a government with bicameral representation with checks and balances. Having both parties represented in the executive branch wasn't quite what Adams had in mind, however, but it did happen in Adams' 1796 election. Adams won 71 electoral votes, and Jefferson won 68, making him the vice president. It was an incredibly close election. To date, this was the only election in the history of the United States where the two top offices were held by individuals from different political parties.

In establishing his Cabinet, Adams selected those who had served during Washington's administration. Historians indicate that Adams wasn't particularly close to any of them but wanted continuity. Jefferson himself was surprised because he knew about the personal attitudes the men in the Cabinet had toward Adams. Most of them were in agreement with the policies of Alexander Hamilton, another Federalist, and sometimes even rejected Adams' input on issues. Jefferson was quoted as having once said, "The Hamiltonians by whom he (Adams) is surrounded are only a little less hostile to him than to me."

The XYZ Affair

In 1793, England and France were at war. France, at that time, was in the hands of the Jacobin party and the National Assembly, establishments that arose during the French Revolution. Because of America's close trade relations with England, Adams wanted to maintain neutrality and avoid being drawn into a war. As he was concerned about how to prevent that, Adams approached Congress in 1797, indicating that American defenses should be strengthened in case of a threat. The Democratic-Republicans reacted negatively to this because they heavily supported the French Republic and didn't want to offend them. However, the Federalists agreed with Adams' precautions and wariness. Once Adams became aware of the possible reaction of France, he wanted to smooth over relations with them, so he sent three peace commissioners over there—Elbridge Gerry, Charles Pinckney, and John Marshall. This maneuver was labeled as a "peace commission," and the details weren't released to the public.

Gerry was a member of the Federalist Party and an exporter from Massachusetts who had familiarity with trade. He was considered a moderate by the Federalists. Charles Pinckney came from a Southern background and was more sensitive to the needs of those who were less fortunate. John Marshall was a staunch conservative and Federalist who believed in a strong central government and preferred Britain over France. In terms of America's public position, he preferred to express neutrality in foreign affairs.

In order to affect a positive outcome for the envoys, Vice President Jefferson met with the French representative in America, Joseph Letombe. He urged Letombe to convince France to spend a long time with the negotiations, saying, "Listen to them and then drag out the negotiations at length and mollify them by the urbanity of the proceedings." Jefferson felt that John Adams would only be a one-term president and thought that France would fare better under a new president, preferably himself. Adams did have a negative view of France, due in part to the treatment he received from them while he was an ambassador. Unfortunately, he made that attitude obvious in a rather bellicose speech to Congress just prior to the departure of his peace delegation.

Upon their arrival in France, the three peace envoys met with Charles Maurice de Talleyrand, the French foreign minister. However, Talleyrand harbored ill feelings toward John Adams, having heard his speech to the US Congress. As a result, Talleyrand met with the American delegation very briefly. He then referred them to three agents who had the code names X, Y, and Z. The French emissaries indicated that they would refrain from hostilities if the US would grant the Republic of France a 12-million-dollar loan, if President Adams apologized for his offensive remarks about France in his speech, and if they made another payment to the avaricious Talleyrand personally.

Adams was incensed and considered that an insult. He publicly announced that the mission was a failure without elucidating any specifics, as he didn't want to create even more friction between the two countries. Then he reiterated his need to strengthen the country's defenses. Because neither Congress nor the public knew why the peace effort had failed, rumors flew about. The Democratic-Republicans, in particular, felt that Adams was hiding positive information related to France because of his prejudice. Congress then required Adams to release the details about the XYZ Affair. When he did so, the Democratic-Republicans were embarrassed, and the American public was shocked. Adams popularity soared to new heights among the public for taking this honest and courageous standpoint. The country's attitudes understandably began to turn against France, and the Federalists sent out anti-French propaganda. Congress was alarmed by the French reaction to the peace mission, and laws were passed that strengthened the United States Army and Navy. Of course, Congress had to raise taxes as well to support that.

John Adams was extremely leery of being responsible for permitting another war to occur so soon after the War of Independence, so he and the Federalist-dominated Congress passed a series of four laws, known as the Alien and Sedition Acts, to prevent the French from having undue influence in America.

The Alien and Sedition Acts

These acts were passed by a narrow margin in 1798 and severely restricted immigration by requiring that a foreigner wait fourteen years before applying for citizenship. In addition, the president was permitted to accuse anyone as being a threat to the security of the United States and had the right to deport him. Any publication that was critical of the US government was also forbidden. Because Adams and many members of his Cabinet were Federalists, those laws also protected them from criticism. The Democratic-Republicans had been weakened after the XYZ Affair, but they felt that the Alien and Sedition Acts were unreasonably harsh. They argued strongly that these laws were unconstitutional because they directly restricted the freedom of speech. Many outrageous arrests were made because of those laws, and notable people from both political parties were imprisoned on scurrilous charges.

For example, Roger Griswold and Matthew Lyon, both of Connecticut, were expelled from the House of Representatives and arrested for sedition. It seems that Griswold, a Federalist, had read some anti-Federalist articles penned by his fellow congressman, Matthew Lyon. At one session in the House, Griswold chased after Lyon with a hickory stick. After catching up to Lyon, Griswold struck him a number of times on his shoulders and head. Lyon then spit tobacco at Griswold in retaliation. Although it's true that they could have been arrested for assault, they were arrested by virtue of the Alien and Sedition Acts. Furthermore, when a man by the name of Anthony Haswell tried to pay the fine for the release of Matthew Lyon, he, too, was arrested!

Likewise, a journalist, Thomas Cooper, went to prison for writing critical articles about Adams. In issuing their verdict, the court said that Cooper was "a person of wicked and turbulent disposition." James Callender was subjected to the same fate when he penned an anti-Federalist pamphlet, *The Prospect Before Us*. Benjamin Franklin Bache, the publisher of the *Philadelphia Aurora*, a newspaper that supported Jeffersonian thoughts, was also arrested for his articles that attacked John Adams. He called him the "old, querulous, bald, blind, crippled, Toothless Adams." Abigail Adams often spoke to her husband about the politics of the day, and she flew into a frenzy when she read words that attacked her husband. She called Bache of the *Aurora* newspaper insolent and abusive and called the man a "lying wretch." Bache was the grandson of Benjamin Franklin, and because of his relationship to the famous scientist, his detractors referred to him as "Lightning Rod Junior."

22 other people were charged under these acts. Usually, these charges represented a devious form of negative politicking rather than true sedition or treason.

Chapter 6 – To Fight or Not to Fight: The Quasi-War

The Quasi-War has been called such because it wasn't a declared war. Due to hostilities with France that had affected America after the XYZ Affair failed in its peace mission, French vessels started attacking American merchant vessels. They were intent upon inspecting the ships for weapons and equipment bound for England and other countries who opposed France during their revolutionary war period (1789-1799). In 1798, just two years into the Adams' administration, Congress approved of hiring privateers to patrol the shore and rescinded all treaties with France. John Adams also proposed that America replenish their navy.

Naval Engagements

James McHenry of Maryland, the secretary of war, authorized 25 American warships to be built. The fear of a war with France was heightened when a French vessel, *La Croyable*, came precariously close to the state of New Jersey. It wasn't a commercial vessel; it was commandeered by privateers. Once that happened, the *La Croyable* was seized off the shores of Egg Harbor, New Jersey, and impounded. *La Croyable* had also been responsible for capturing a British merchant vessel earlier along with one owned by a Philadelphia company.

On the high seas, the USS *Constellation* engaged the French ship *La Vengeance* in the vicinity of the West Indies as it headed toward America's southern shore. The French ship was actually heading back to France with passengers, but the signal flags hoisted by the two ships weren't understood, and the USS *Constellation* gave chase. Captain Thomas Truxton of the *Constellation* demanded surrender, but the French refused. Both ships opened fire. In the half-light of the reflection from gunfire, the USS *Constellation* lost its rigging, and *La Vengeance* limped its way to Curacao where the French captain was forced to beach her.

More than a dozen US merchant vessels were attacked by the French during 1798. Only one American ship was seized, the *Retaliation*, which was outgunned by two French warships. The captain, William Bainbridge, was detained at the French island of Guadeloupe in the West Indies. Governor Victor Hugues of that island wanted to preserve trade and be guaranteed neutrality, so he attempted to bargain with Bainbridge. However, Bainbridge knew that the American seamen who had been captured by the French before this had been mistreated, and he used this incident to draw attention to that. Instead of cooperating with the French authorities on the island, he protested, knowing it would reach the national media. In addition, he indicated to the French that he wasn't authorized to grant neutrality. Since the French governor was sincere, he released the American sailors that the island held, including Bainbridge. Hugues then sent a communique to President Adams. That letter, though, was accompanied with the threat that should their neutrality proposal be denied, any American sailors found off their shores would be executed.

To continue in their efforts to protect American shipping interest in other areas of the Caribbean, the USS *Merrimack* was launched by the noteworthy shipbuilders of Newburyport, Massachusetts, for service in 1799. She was tasked with escorting American merchant ships, and as one of its first actions, the *Merrimack* captured *L'Magicienne*, the former *Retaliation*, outside of the Caribbean. In naval warfare, it was fairly common to seize enemy ships and refit them for use by one's own navy. Following that, the USS *Merrimack* took the French ships *Bonaparte 7, Ganges,* the *Phoenix, Ceres,* the *Brilliant*, and the schooners *John* and *Godfrey*, the latter of which was the property of the British navy.

Armed Forces and Political Strife

Without approaching George Washington, Adams appointed him the head of the ground forces in this Quasi-War. Washington was then 67 years old and retired. He graciously accepted, but he didn't feel physically capable of adequately serving in the role of commander-in-chief at that age. He accepted Adams' appointment for the sake of the country but added the caveat that he must be free to choose his own leaders or he wouldn't take the post. The former president was given permission to do so, and he chose Alexander Hamilton, a man that Adams distrusted, to do the actual work involved in organizing and managing the army. John Adams had initially wanted two Democratic-Republicans to fill the associate positions in order to maintain a balance in political factions, but the vociferous Federalists in Congress objected to that. Adams reluctantly relented because his dear wife Abigail was ill, and Adams wasn't prepared for a political battle on top of the stress he was already dealing with.

Besides Alexander Hamilton, Washington selected Charles Pinckney, James McHenry, and Henry Knox to be his top advisors. McHenry declined the position, but the other two men were anxious to fill the roles. Washington, who had suffered from a perennial lack of supplies during the War of Independence, stressed that Alexander Hamilton should be sure that his soldiers had sufficient supplies. As it so happened, there was no ground war phase of the Quasi-War, but it helped to establish the precedent that Congress needed to appoint someone to make arrangements for military equipment, uniforms, and supplies. That would require more taxation, and Adams' administration imposed the Direct House Tax of 1798, which was essentially a property tax. It might come as no surprise that Adams became very unpopular because of it.

John Fries Rebellion

The Direct House Tax of 1798 was levied upon individuals' buildings based upon the number of windows and their land. In the 18th century, glass was expensive because it had to be imported, and people whose homes had more windows were usually wealthier. Tax assessors were sent to the states, but they encountered a great deal of resistance from the people living just outside Philadelphia. When the assessors arrived, the inhabitants ridiculed them and forced them off their property. John Fries, an auctioneer in Pennsylvania, had a general impression about the reactions of the people of his own state because of his occupation and helped to instigate an uprising. Fries held town meetings, prompting the farmers of the area to hold rallies and protest. Having been incensed by the new taxes, the farmers harassed the assessors, and the people of the state itself called upon their local militias to arm themselves and drive the assessors away.

In January of 1799, the US Marshal was sent by the federal government to Pennsylvania, armed with arrest warrants. He located twelve men who were responsible for tax resistance and arrested them. He then had them transported to a temporary jail in Bethlehem, Pennsylvania. The next day, 400 armed men, led by John Fries, arrived at the jail. To quell the crowd, the marshal released a few men as a sign of good faith and started negotiating with Fries.

In response to this action though, President Adams issued orders to the Pennsylvania state militia to march over there and stop the insurrection. When they arrived, they promptly arrested John Fries and 31 others. Those men were jailed in Philadelphia and charged with treason—an offense that might result in execution. According to the law, an attempt to resist the enforcement of a federal law was the same as waging war against the United States. Most of them were released after a short period, except for John Fries and two others who were charged with treason.

Their trial was held in April of 1799, and Fries and the other two men were convicted of treason and sentenced to hang. However, a mistrial was declared when one of the jurors admitted that he had decided ahead of time that they should be hanged.

In 1800, another trial was held. The judge, Richard Peters, and Supreme Court Justice Samuel Chase presided at the trial. At this trial, Fries and the others were once again found guilty of treason and were sentenced to be hanged. However, John Adams pardoned them. Alexander Hamilton was confused by the pardon and responded angrily by saying that it was the "most inexplicable part of Mr. Adams' conduct." When it was published, that statement created a rift in the Federalist Party because it gave rise to arguments amongst the party members themselves.

End of the Quasi-War

By the spring of 1799, the French had let up on their intensive attacks on American ships due to the French losses that occurred overseas during their engagement in the revolutionary wars. In addition, the political landscape had shifted in France, and their focus turned toward internal events. In November of 1799, Napoleon Bonaparte—a former naval commander—staged a coup d'état and took over France. Consequently, the naval battles with America were of little interest, and France announced they wanted to make peace with America.

In his role as the head of France, Napoleon Bonaparte made a lot of reforms and wanted to end the Quasi-War with America. Alexander Hamilton was a presumptuous man, and when he heard about Bonaparte's overtures for peace, he rushed over unannounced to see Adams. Hamilton wanted to convince him to forego a treaty and simply create an alliance with Britain to restore the influence of the Bourbons, who were the ancestors of King Louis XVI, the king the French had violently executed during their revolution. Adams was amused by that, and in his papers, he said, "I heard him with perfect good humor, though never in my life did I hear a man talk more like a fool."

On September 30, 1800, his envoys—Oliver Ellsworth, William Davie, and their leader, William Vans Murray—signed the Treaty of Mortefontaine on behalf of the United States, putting an end to the Quasi-War. The old Treaty of Alliance and Amity between the United States and France in 1778 had already been rescinded at the start of the Quasi-War, but it was now permanently terminated.

Political Rancor

Alexander Hamilton continued to fuel the tensions within the Federalist Party because of his overwhelming need to control its direction. He had many followers but managed to make a number of political enemies. James McHenry, the secretary of war, was one of them.

Further differences arose among the Federalists because of an argument between Adams and McHenry where Adams impulsively fired McHenry. Adams also took that opportunity to ask Timothy Pickering, the secretary of state, to resign. Pickering, it was later discovered, was opposed to making peace with France, and he was in office during the negotiations over the Treaty of Mortefontaine. Pickering adamantly refused to leave, so Adams dismissed him outright and replaced him with John Marshall, the man he wanted to take McHenry's place. The position of secretary of war went to Samuel Dexter instead. The Federalists were, indeed, becoming fractured over policy differences.

Judicial Appointments

In 1798, John Adams appointed Bushrod Washington as an associate justice of the Supreme Court. Adams originally asked John Marshall to serve, but Marshall was running against a Democratic-Republican, John Clopton, in Congress as one of the representatives for Virginia. Marshall won the majority of votes in that race even though he was a member of the Federalist Party—a party that usually wasn't popular in the Southern states.

Bushrod was a friend of Marshall's and was, therefore, Adams' second choice. This was a recess appointment: that is, an appointment made while Congress wasn't in session. Normally, Congress must approve of judicial appointments, but the Constitution states that the president has that power if Congress is in recess. After Congress reconvenes, they are then expected to vote for the continuance or discontinuance of the appointment. Recess appointments became a stumbling block for many US presidents as time went on.

Alfred Moore served on the Supreme Court from 1800 to 1804. He replaced Justice James Iredell, from Washington's administration, who had retired. Most historians indicate that Moore's service was unremarkable, but he was also a sickly man who served for only five years.

In 1800, Adams approached John Jay to serve as the chief justice after the resignation of Oliver Ellsworth, who had become extremely ill. However, John Jay, who had been the first chief justice of the Supreme Court, turned down Adams' appointment. John Jay had become disgusted with party politics during the year of 1800, and he was particularly incensed when Hamilton tried to manipulate the electoral laws. Jay was a "purist," meaning he believed that the political process should be honorable and that both appointments and elections should be decided by the people without undue influence.

After Jay declined the appointment, Adams sought out his secretary of state, John Marshall, to assume the position. Marshall served out his role as secretary of state and then assumed the position of chief justice after Adams left office. Marshall was perhaps one of the most learned men in the justice department and authored many books. As chief justice, he altered the way the Supreme Court did business. Up until 1800, the Supreme Court was very much like a traveling circuit court. However, as cases became more complex and involved constitutional matters, Marshall saw to it that the Supreme Court operated independently.

Chapter 7 – 1800: The Politics of Dissension

The Capitol of the United States

In 1790, Congress had approved of the building of the United States Capitol. By 1800, many of the buildings had been erected, and John Adams was the first president to reside in the President's Mansion which resided on a small hill in the center of the city. This mansion was later renamed by the more recognizable name of the White House. Nearby stood Congress Hall, which later became the United States Capitol building. Pierre (or Peter, as he went by that name in the United States) Charles L'Enfant designed the city itself, while Dr. William Thornton and Stephen Hallett were the architects of the United States Capitol. James Hoban, an architect from Ireland, was chosen to design the President's Mansion. The architects were awarded the positions in a competition held during George Washington's presidency.

John Adams visited some of the nearly completed buildings in 1800 as he readied himself for the upcoming presidential campaign. He and Abigail moved into the President's Mansion in the late fall of that year just as the campaign was heating up.

Political Warriors

The campaign for the election of 1800 was one of the most contentious of 19th-century America. The rivalry of the two political parties—the Federalist and Democratic-Republican Parties—was malicious and negative. Throughout the campaign, wild rumors flourished, much to the titillation of American readers, and many believed them.

Thomas Jefferson and Aaron Burr of the Democratic-Republican Party ran against Adams. Jefferson was convinced that the Federalist Party betrayed the cause of liberty by granting too much power to the national government. He was a champion of states' rights and felt that a strong central government would be oppressive. Aaron Burr was very popular in New York politics, and that helped him win room on the ticket. He and Jefferson were an unlikely pair, though, as Burr was heavily involved in banking. Jefferson himself had a negative opinion of banks and associated them with the wealthy aristocracy.

John Adams was one of the Federalist candidates along with Charles C. Pickney of South Carolina. Charles Cotesworth Pinckney was known to the people as one of the agents sent by Adams to negotiate the failed XYZ Affair. After his return from France, he became disillusioned with the French in general but came across as a political moderate. Because he was a Southerner and had military experience (unlike Adams), the party felt that he might be successful as a candidate.

As soon the political battle formations were drawn up, the rumor mill started grinding. Because of Adams' aristocratic mannerisms, one rumor stated that Adams was plotting to have his son, John Quincy Adams, marry a daughter of King George III. The Federalists, on the other hand, cast Jefferson as a pro-French radical, saying that he would carry on a Reign of Terror, much like Robespierre did under the French Republic. The smear campaign that was conducted is uncomfortably similar to the campaigns of today in which each side attempts to hurl accusations at the other regardless of their validity.

What's more, the debt from the Quasi-War was tremendous because America had taken out a lot of loans to build their navy. As a result of the Direct House Tax of 1789, many Americans fell into economic hardships. Although Democratic-Republicans had encouraged the Quasi-War, that was quickly forgotten when they stirred the public's emotions with incessant propaganda against the reelection of John Adams. His political enemy and fellow Federalist, Alexander Hamilton, wasted no time in disparaging Adams. During the course of Adams' campaign, he wrote an inflammatory letter to some electors. Although decorated in elaborate and heavily tailored terms, he inserted comments like:

> Mr. Adams has committed some serious errors of administration; that in addition to these, he has certain fixed points of character which tend naturally to the detriment of any cause of which he is the chief; that he has furnished deadly weapons to its enemies by unfounded accusations, and has weakened the force of its friends.

Some Federalists urged Hamilton not to send the letter, but he ignored their advice. Hamilton followed that letter up with a pamphlet denouncing Adams' decisions to discharge Pickering and McHenry. In addition, Hamilton suggested that the electors should vote for Charles Pinckney, the other Federalist running against Adams.

Adams wasn't the only one that Hamilton harbored ill will toward. He also disliked Aaron Burr, just as Burr did him. Now that he was Jefferson's running mate, it inflamed their antipathy toward each other. Burr reportedly saw to it that Hamilton's otherwise private letter to the electors was made public; Hamilton had originally planned on just a public release of his follow-up pamphlet against John Adams. Their rivalry contributed to divisions within the Federalist Party.

In 1800, William Duane, who had taken over the *Philadelphia Aurora* after Bache, published a letter written to Tench Coxe that said there were still men influenced by Great Britain in the US government. The letter was private, but somehow, it was revealed. Adams was not just embarrassed; he was furious. The whole intent of the letter had been taken out of context and written in such a way as to imply that Adams himself had some degree of loyalty to Great Britain. Word spread that Duane was also being sought by authorities who wanted to charge him under the Alien and Sedition Acts. As a result, Jefferson interceded, indicating Duane had to be let out until he could find an attorney. After that, Duane went into hiding until the end of Adams' administration.

It was hard for the public to relate to Adams, even without slanderous words being printed against his character. Abigail and John liked to travel in style, even though Adams wasn't really considered all that wealthy. He and Abigail enjoyed the pomp and circumstance, and that led to a lot of criticism related to their being aristocrats and monarchists. In 1799, when they were traveling in their entourage through New Jersey, ceremonial cannons were fired as a salute. Hearing that, Luther Baldwin, the driver of a garbage scow in Newark, New Jersey, rushed out from a local tavern, shouting, "There goes the president and they are firing at his arse!" He then followed that up with the comment, "I do not care if they fire thro' his arse!" As expected, he was arrested then convicted and imprisoned on the charge that he spoke "seditious words tending to defame the president and the government of the United States."

Election Results and Ramifications

This election was different than the elections before as the voting regulations had changed. Five states now allowed qualified voters to vote for the federal electors. That number had been seven in the 1796 election. The other states adopted a "winner-take-all" system, also called plurality-at-large voting. At-large voting means that a representative is elected to vote for a district, town, or state; this was banned in 1842, as it was determined to be biased and could lead to gerrymandering, a system in which districts are split in such a way as to favor certain candidates.

It is possible this new system didn't aid John Adams and Charles Pinckney, who both lost the election. Charles Pinckney received the least number of votes of all the candidates (64); however, Adams only gained one more vote than Pinckney. Thomas Jefferson and Aaron Burr were tied at a vote of 73-73. In that case, the Constitution stipulated that the winner must be selected by the House of Representatives. Each state represented in the House had one vote, and a supermajority determined the outcome. The final vote came to 10-4 in favor of Jefferson.

After this vicious and slanderous campaign, the Federalist Party started to disintegrate. Analysts say the split was due to the antipathy of Hamilton and Adams. In addition, political thinkers indicate that the platform of the Federalist Party eventually evolved into that of today's Republican Party, and the Democratic-Republicans, who actually referred to themselves as the Republican Party back then (the name Democratic-Republicans is used to differentiate themselves from the current Republicans), became the current-day Democrats.

Shortly after taking office, Thomas Jefferson released everyone who had been imprisoned under the Alien and Sedition Acts and gave them an official apology. In 1800, the Alien and Sedition Acts expired, although a segment called the Alien Enemies Act remains in effect to this day. This act allows for an alien to be deported if he or she is determined to be dangerous to the nation's security during a war.

Chapter 8 – John Adams: His Thoughts and Retirement

Back to Old Peacefield

John Adams was a farmer at heart, so he wasn't crushed by having lost his bid for another term as president. John Adams' son, Charles, who had accompanied him on his ambassadorship in Paris, achieved a bad reputation while attending Harvard University because he became an alcoholic who was often involved in drunken antics on campus. Following his graduation, he passed the bar and apprenticed briefly under Alexander Hamilton. After that, Charles borrowed a lot of money from his father, presumably to open up a law practice. However, he squandered the money and abandoned his wife, Sarah, and his two daughters, Susanna and Abigail. In 1798, John felt that Charles was a "madman possessed of the devil" and disowned him. Charles died of cirrhosis of the liver in 1800. When John and Abigail retired to Peacefield, they welcomed Charles' wife and their daughters to live with them.

John Quincy Adams lived nearby with his wife and children. He visited his parents quite frequently and often stayed with them for weeks on end. It was convenient for John Quincy because he had entered politics in Massachusetts.

Attitude on Slavery

In 1801, two fervent abolitionists—George Churchman and Jacob Lindley—sent John Adams a letter, enclosing a copy of Warner Mifflin's late 18th-century pamphlet against slavery. As a Quaker, Mifflin didn't condone slavery and spent most of his life campaigning against the practice. As part of his campaign against slavery, Mifflin sent out pamphlets and letters to the influential politicians of the day.

George Churchman was a Pennsylvanian Quaker who opened Quaker schools and promoted the education of women as well as men. Jacob Lindley, also from Pennsylvania, was a Presbyterian minister who served as a missionary in Africa and later became the first president of Ohio University.

John Adams responded to the letter by saying:

> Although I have never sought popularity by any animated speeches or inflammatory publications against the slavery of Blacks, my opinion against it has always been known and my practice has been so conformable to my sentiment that I have always employed freemen both as domestics and laborers, and never in my life did I own a slave.

Because John Adams wasn't extremely vocal about his stance against slavery, Mifflin and Churchman were unaware of it. Adams, knowing that slavery was a divisive issue, tended to avoid bringing it up.

In 1822, he wrote to Thomas Pickering, expressing his disappointment that the Constitution of the United States did not abolish slavery. It had appeared in an earlier draft of the Constitution, but it was ultimately rejected in the final version.

John Adams believed in a gradual transition in order to free the country from the evils of slavery. Because of the economic dependency of the South upon slavery, he felt that sudden emancipation would be not only a divisive issue but also a traumatic one as well.

The Rise of His Son

John Adams' son, John Quincy Adams, followed in his father's footsteps by becoming a lawyer and then entering the field of politics. After having lost the 1800 election, John Adams was gratified to learn that his own son had been elected as a senator of Massachusetts. Like his father, he was also a Federalist, but he became disenchanted with that party and became a Democratic-Republican later in life. He also befriended James Madison, who appointed him as an ambassador to Russia. In addition, he also served as an ambassador to England as his father did. By 1817, John Quincy Adams became secretary of state under President James Monroe, and in 1825, he even became president, a year before his father died.

Adams on Monarchy

Adams was often criticized for favoring a monarchical form of government, but he rejected the opinions of those who said he felt positively about monarchies. In a letter to Thomas Jefferson, he said he never promoted such a thing and challenged anyone who could find evidence to the contrary. However, a critical reading of his documents appears to show ambiguity with regard to the "aristocracy." For example, in 1779, when formulating the state constitution for Massachusetts, he said, "We have so many men of wealth, of ambitious spirits, or intrigue, of luxury and corruption, that incessant factions will disturb our peace without it." Adams was referring to the powers of the three branches of government, but he felt that there should be one individual bestowed with power over all three branches. Without that person, Adams felt that the government would "be run down like a hare before the hunters." As for the Governor's Council, Adams preferred that the members of such a council had the right to approve or reject appointments related to civil, judicial, and military positions. Despite his respect for a more "elite" composition of that council, he manifested some fears about the control of a republican form of government by aristocracies, especially new ones. Adams intensely disliked some of the emotional corruption of politicians but said that "There are as many and as dangerous aristocratical demagogues as there are democratical."

He seems to have ended up with a contradictory concept about the structure of a government. On the one hand, he had an antipathy toward the oligarchy of the rich classes who would deprive the people of their rights but also suggested that the upper echelon of society be curbed by a strong executive. Curiously, the result could be just the same; only the doer would change.

Adams did feel, however, that monarchies historically outlived democracies. He is quoted as saying, "Remember, democracy never lasts long. It soon wastes, exhausts and murders itself. There never was a democracy yet that does not commit suicide."

Literary Endeavor: *In Defense of Constitutions*

Adams wrote a 3-volume series while abroad called *In Defense of Constitutions* in 1787. In it, Adams delineates the various forms of governments, even including those in ancient times. It contains a survey and discussion of various types of governmental republics from history and went on to espouse political philosophies from the past, like those of Anne Robert Turgot and Richard Price, who were both accomplished statesmen and writers. One of the reasons John Adams explored the structure of governments is that, unlike today, there were no contemporary democracies or democratic republics upon which to model a new government that would work for America. The United States wasn't set up as a pure democracy anyway, and the founders recognized that. The Founders intended it to be a democratic republic. Adams said that if all men were able to follow natural law, a government would be unnecessary. However, people are subject to their passions, and such unbridled freedom would invite abuse without the law.

James Madison, who helped to write the Constitution, based his writing upon the recommendations of the delegates of the Constitutional Convention; he personally defined democracy as a "pure democracy," meaning "a society consisting of a small number of citizens to assemble and administer the government in person." To Madison, a republic yielded "a government in which the scheme of representation takes place." That is, the people elected representatives who, in turn, administered the government. It is noteworthy that Madison never applied the term "democracy" to the government of America. He preferred to use the term "republic."

There was some confusion as to the definition of "republic" anyway. To Adams, the term "republic" meant:

> Could be no other than a government in which the property of the people predominated and governed; and it had more relation to property than liberty. It signified a government in which the property of the public, or people, and of every one of them, was secured and protected by law.

Adams emphasized the law to be the external factor that guided the actions of all, including the people elected to office. He felt that civil law was absolutely necessary as a mechanism to restrain men from falling upon their natural weaknesses, regardless of their posts or positions within the structure. However, Adams modified the concept that men must be subject to the law to mean that there should be sufficient flexibility so that they are not slaves to its literal interpretation. In addition, he stressed the fact that any law needs to be a "good law" and that it protects both the majority and the minority. He said that "laws are neither made by angels, nor by horses" and that there needs to be a system of checks and balances in place.

Historians have criticized *In Defense of Constitutions* as being too voluminous and mostly paraphrased or quoted from other sources. Only the last few essays or "letters," as they were called, appear to have sprung from Adams' own thoughts. Although Adams was complimented on some of the scholarly material in the beginning, political writers called the huge series "incoherent" and "disorganized." Adams did have a tendency to start on a project, heavily invest his mind into it, but then either leave it unfinished or unedited, which is what may have happened with this work. He also never finished his own autobiography.

Adams Reconciles with Jefferson

Thomas Jefferson and John Adams had been on a friendly basis during the initial years of America. They had worked together on the content of the Declaration of Independence and had even communicated with each other when Jefferson was the American ambassador to France in 1785 and Adams was the country's ambassador to England. However, the two political parties of the nation—the Federalists and the Democratic-Republicans—became more widely disparate, and Adams and Jefferson had grown apart. Jefferson's on-going support of France, even during their revolutionary war period, was another bone of contention between them. The tumultuous election of 1800 played a very strong role in driving these two idealistic and committed patriots apart even further.

At one point, Abigail wrote a letter of sympathy to Thomas Jefferson on the death of his daughter, Polly. In his response, though, Jefferson threw out a barb toward Adams about his "unkind appointment" of federal judges toward the end of his presidency but said he "forgave" him for it. Judges appointed just as a president was leaving office were called "midnight judges," and at the time, they weren't subject to congressional approval. Abigail, still stinging from the slander spread during Jefferson's campaign, retorted with annoyance over that.

Benjamin Rush, a physician and signer of the Declaration of Independence, wanted to reunite the two and wrote a number of letters to both of them. John Adams was the first to break the ice. In 1812, he wrote to Jefferson, saying, "Madame joins and sends her kind regards to your daughter and your grandchildren as well as to yourself." Jefferson speedily replied. After that, Adams wrote to Jefferson, "You and I ought not to die before we have explained ourselves to each other." That they did, and they more calmly discussed the political implications of America, including those issues upon which they differed. The pair exchanged about 158 letters after their reconciliation.

John Adams developed heart disease but lived for many years after the diagnosis. He died of congestive heart failure at the age of 91. It is curious to note that both John Adams and Thomas Jefferson died on Independence Day, July 4, of 1826. Adams' last words were "Jefferson still lives," but he was wrong by about five hours.

Conclusion

John Adams lived through one of the most difficult times in early America. His presidential predecessor, George Washington, had fame thrust upon him because of his contribution in winning the American War of Independence. When Adams came into office, America was heavily conflicted politically and financially. War became a distinct possibility while America was still undergoing growing pains. Adams successfully kept the nation from becoming involved in another war, but he is rarely given credit for that.

Prior to his tenure as president, Adams was placed in the position of ambassador more than once but became frustrated due to the failure of the Continental Congress to set up a workable system of laws to back him up. Although he was sometimes described as being "abrasive," the uncomfortable situations with which he had to deal with would try the patience of any reasonable man. Adams was a lawyer who had a sharp mind and could destroy opponents by pointing out the contradictions in their own arguments. Honesty was perhaps the strongest of all his traits. During the XYZ Affair, he adamantly refused to accept bribes, even though they may have resolved the differences between France and the United States.

Because Adams raised taxes during his presidency, he became extremely unpopular during his administration. However, he had seen unhappy results when a young nation is insufficiently financed and forced to depend upon other countries, which could lead to undesirable entanglements. America gained a navy and an army as a result of those taxes and now had the means to maintain its integrity and independence, as well as gain the respect of other nations.

He was a firm believer in the balance of power within the government. Long before it was written into the Constitution, Adams promoted the separation of the government into three branches—the executive, legislative, and judicial. That separation of powers proved to be one of John Adams' greatest insights, as it was written into the final US Constitution, which was ratified in 1788. During the preliminary discussions on the Constitution, the issue of the abolition of slavery had arisen, but feelings on the issue were mixed, so it wasn't included. With regard to John Adams, he was one of the few Founding Fathers who never owned a slave. Instead of succumbing to the economic advantage of having free labor on his farm, he insisted on hiring only freemen to assist him.

John Adams had the honor of having a son, John Quincy Adams, who also became president of the United States, serving from 1825-1829. Only he and George H.W. Bush (1989-1993) had sons who also became a president.

Read more biographies from Captivating History

References

Adams, J. and Adams, C. (1851) *The Works of John Adams, Second President of the United States.* Little, Brown and Company

Adams, J. (author), Wroth, L and Zobel, H. (eds.) (1965) *The Legal Papers of John Adams.* Harvard University Press

"Adams Family Papers," Retrieved from
http://www.masshist.org/adams/adams-family-papers

"Adams Campaigns and Election," Retrieved from
https://millercenter.org/president/adams/campaigns-and-elections

Anderson, B. "John Adams: A Liberal Congregationalist and the American Revolution," Retrieved from
https://allthingsliberty.com/2018/06/john-adams-a-liberal-congregationalist-and-the-american-revolution/

"Boston Tea Party," Retrieved from
https://www.bostonteapartyship.com/john-adams-diplomat-france

Chinard, G. (1933) *Honest John Adams.* Little, Brown and Company

Diggins, J. (author) and Arthur M. Schlesinger, Jr. (ed.) (2003) *John Adams: The American Presidents Series: The 2nd President, 1797-1801*. Macmillan

"The Dutch Loan," Retrieved from
https://www.johnadams.us/p/dutch-loan.html

Ferling, J. (1992) *John Adams: A Life.* University of Tennessee Press

Green, J. "The Discourses on Davila," Retrieved from https://presidentialfellows.wordpress.com/2012/03/20/john-adams-discourses-on-davila/ "The Center for the Study of the Presidency and Congress,"

Harmon, T. "How an Earlier Patriot Law Brought Down a President," Retrieved from https://www.bigeye.com/hartmann.htm

"Humphrey Ploughjogger to the Boston Gazette, 14 October 1765," Retrieved from
https://founders.archives.gov/documents/Adams/06-01-02-0057

"John Adams and the Massachusetts Constitution," Retrieved from
https://www.mass.gov/guides/john-adams-the-massachusetts-constitution

McCullough, D. (2001) *John Adams.* Simon Schuster

"Our Documents: The Judiciary," Retrieved from
https://www.loc.gov/rr/program/bib/ourdocs/judiciary.html

Pollard, E. (1862) *The First Year of the War.* West & Johnson

"The Quasi-War, America's First Limited War," Retrieved from https://www.cnrs-scrn.org/northern_mariner/vol18/tnm_18_3-4_67-77.pdf

Ragsdale, B. "The Sedition Act Trials," Retrieved from
https://www.fjc.gov/sites/default/files/trials/seditionacts.pdf

Ryerson et. al. (eds.) (1993) *Adams Family Correspondence, Vol 5.* The Belknap Press of Harvard University

Ryerson, R. (2016) *John Adams's Republic: The One, the Few, and the Many.* JHU Press

Smith P. (1962) *John Adams, Vols. 1 and II.* W.W. Norton

Wood, G. (2017) *Empire of Liberty: A History of the Early Republic.* Oxford University Press

www.ingramcontent.com/pod-product-compliance
Lightning Source LLC
LaVergne TN
LVHW090036080526
838202LV00046B/3838